BOXING

The Greatest Fighters of the 20th Century

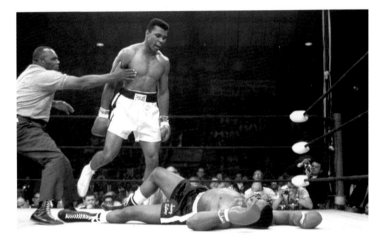

BOXING

The Greatest Fighters of the 20th Century

Chris King

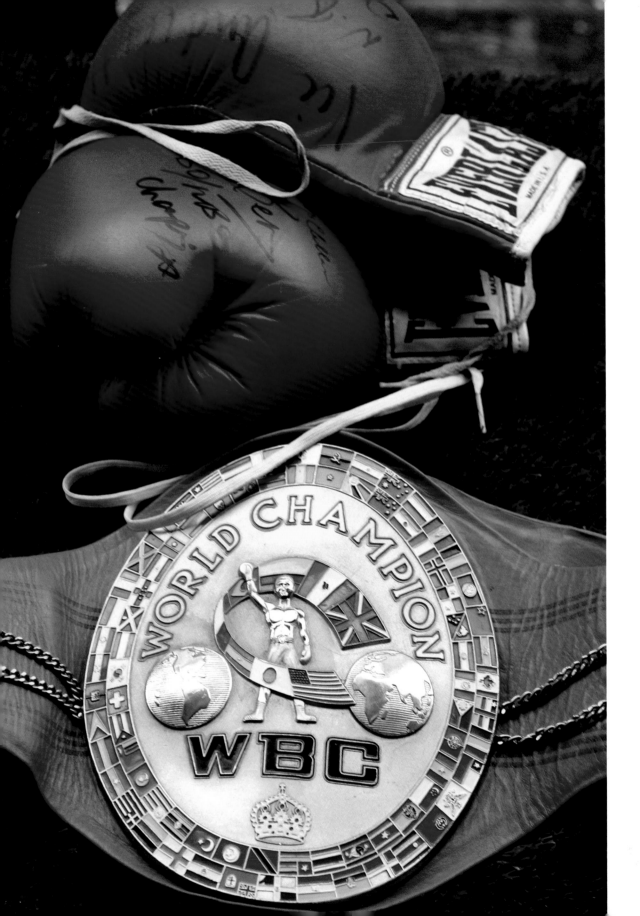

This edition is published by Lorenz Books
an imprint of Anness Publishing Ltd
Blaby Road, Wigston
Leicestershire LE18 4SE
info@anness.com

www.lorenzbooks.com
www.annesspublishing.com

Anness Publishing has a new picture
agency outlet for images for publishing,
promotions or advertising. Please visit
our website www.practicalpictures.com
for more information.

A CIP catalogue record for this book
is available from the British Library.

Publisher: Joanna Lorenz
Produced by Editorial Developments,
  Edgmond, Shropshire, England
Designer: Chensie Chen
Index: Q C Daniel, Arundel
Production Controller: Wendy Lawson

PUBLISHER'S NOTE
Although the information in this book is
believed to be accurate and true at the
time of going to press, neither the authors
nor the publisher can accept any legal
responsibility or liability for any errors
or omissions that may have been made.

Page 1: Muhammad Ali and Sonny Liston.
*Pages 2–3: Ricky Hatton and Floyd
Mayweather Jr.*
*Page 4: World Boxing Council championship
belt and gloves.*
Page 5: Sugar Shane Mosley.

Contents

The Early History

This Minoan fresco found on the island of Santorini depicts two boys boxing. It is around 3,600 years old. Another boxing fresco was found at the Minoan palace of Knossos.

It is impossible to know for certain when the first boxing match took place. However, we have evidence for the sport's existence in many of the world's great early civilizations. A fresco in the Minoan palace at Knossos in Crete shows two young boxers with their hands bound in leather thongs, while similar pictorial evidence proves that the sport flourished in ancient Iraq and Egypt. Boxing was extremely popular in ancient Greece, where it was an Olympic sport from 688BC onwards. From Greece, the sport spread to Rome, where fighters battled in the gladiatorial arenas with spiked iron gloves.

Modern boxing's origins lie in England, where most of the principles that shape today's sport were established. However, early boxing matches differed considerably from the contests that we are familiar with today. Wrestling holds and throws were permitted and contests generally went on until one of the fighters could no longer continue. In addition, no gloves were worn; for this reason this period of the sport's history is known as the bare knuckle era.

Boxing's first champion is generally regarded to be James Figg, who was born around 1695. Figg styled himself a "master of the noble science of defence", an art that he taught to aristocratic patrons at his school in London. Figg became the self-declared champion of England in 1719 and over the next 15 years fought a series of contests against challengers from all over the country. Figg was not only a master of fighting with his fists; at his school he also taught the use of a variety of weapons and would accept challenges in these arts as well. For example, he fought one rival, Ned Sutton, with fists, swords and cudgels, defeating him in each discipline.

Over the course of his reign, Figg boxed against countless rivals, sometimes at his school, which was

James Figg, portrayed here in a nineteenth-century illustration, is often seen as the father of modern boxing. Figg was England's first ever heavyweight champion.

6

Like Figg, Broughton was a master fencer, and he used his knowledge of the art to develop a more scientific approach to the sport of boxing, parrying and blocking blows before counterattacking.

In 1741 Broughton took part in a contest that would change the course of the sport of boxing. The fight, which took place near Tottenham Court Road, London, pitted Broughton against the Yorkshireman George Stevenson. Broughton's greater power enabled him to overcome his quicker adversary and the injuries Stevenson sustained eventually cost him his life. In response, Broughton took it upon himself to devise a set of rules to protect boxers.

Broughton's Rules were introduced in 1743, the same year that he established his own boxing amphitheatre.

This trade card designed by the English artist William Hogarth advertises the boxing school run by James Figg. Also a master fencer, Figg taught both armed and unarmed combat.

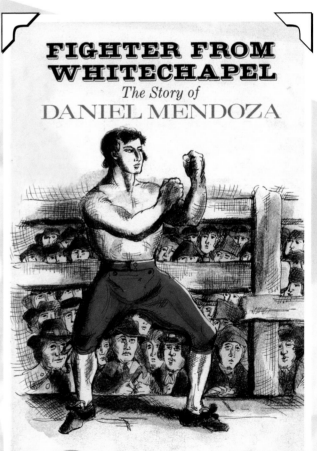

FIGHTER FROM WHITECHAPEL
The Story of
DANIEL MENDOZA

by Harold U. Ribalow
illustrated by SIMON JERUCHIM

known as Figg's Amphitheatre, and sometimes at Southwark Fair, where he took on all comers. Figg's fame was such that he mingled with high society, becoming an acquaintance of the Prince of Wales.

When Figg retired in 1734, the title of champion of England passed to one of his pupils, George Taylor, who held it until 1738, when he lost a contest to Jack Broughton, a muscular fighter who worked as a waterman, rowing passengers across the Thames River.

One of the most skilful fighters of his era, Daniel Mendoza frequently defeated larger and stronger opponents. He became a considerable celebrity in eighteenth-century London.

Butcher   Johnson   MENDOZA   WARD   Joe Ward   Jackson

Although the rules were initially drawn up to govern contests that took place in his venue, they eventually became the standard set of regulations governing the sport. The rules stipulated that every time a man was thrown or knocked down, he would have 30 seconds to make it back to a square at the centre of the ring, where he would stand face to face with his opponent. His opponent would not be allowed to strike until he made it back to the centre of the ring. When a fighter could not make it back to the square, he would be deemed the loser. Further rules banned striking a fighter while he was on one knee and grabbing him by the legs.

Broughton's reign ended in 1750 when he was defeated by the Norwich butcher Jack Slack. Broughton was forced to retire when a punch temporarily blinded him, a decision that enraged his patron, the Duke of Cumberland, who had thousands of pounds riding on the outcome of the contest. Cumberland withdrew his financial support, forcing Broughton to give up fighting.

The title of champion of England continued to change hands over the course of the eighteenth century, with the holder of the title enjoying considerable celebrity. One such boxer was Daniel Mendoza, a small fighter who used speed of footwork to bewilder larger and clumsier fighters. Mendoza eventually lost his title in 1795 to "Gentleman" John Jackson, who won with a controversial tactic, holding Mendoza's hair with one hand while pounding his face with the other. Jackson retired immediately after his title fight, but contributed to the development of boxing in another way by

Daniel Mendoza (left) holds William Ward in a headlock during the course of one of the pair's two encounters. Wrestling holds such as this were a common part of bare knuckle fights.

founding the Pugilistic Society, which sought to organize and regulate the sport.

In the early nineteenth century, bare knuckle fighting entered a golden age in terms of popularity. The most celebrated encounters of this era occurred between the English fighter Tom Cribb and two African-Americans, Bill Richmond and Tom Molineaux. Richmond was born a slave on Staten Island, New York, where his fighting prowess caught the attention of General Percy, Duke of Northumberland. Percy took him on as his servant and brought him to England where he took part in a series of bouts while working as a carpenter. Richmond gained a reputation as a quick and skilful fighter whose technique made up for his lack of size and strength.

In 1805, Richmond, now a veteran of 42, was matched against the younger, bigger and stronger Tom Cribb. Cribb had built up a reputation as a fighter while working as a stevedore on the wharves of London and had just started boxing professionally. His fight against Richmond lasted 90 minutes, and eventually Cribb's greater strength won the day. Cribb followed up the victory with several other high-profile wins, including two against former champion Jem Belcher. When the current holder of the English title, John Gully, retired in 1808, Cribb was hailed as champion in his wake.

The illustration on this jug depicts the fight between the Englishman Tom Cribb and the former slave Tom Molineaux. The contest took place in 1810 and resulted in a victory for Cribb.

An immigrant from Ireland, James "Yankee" Sullivan was a popular prize fighter in nineteenth-century America. He is best known for his contest against Tom Hyer in 1849.

The boxer John C. Heenan claimed the title "heavyweight champion of America" in 1859. He later crossed the Atlantic to fight the English champion Tom Sayers.

Bill Richmond's exploits inspired another African-American to try his hand in the English prize rings. Tom Molineaux had been pitted against his fellow slaves by plantation owners in his native Virginia. Before one such contest (on which a large amount of money had been wagered), Molineaux's master had promised him his freedom if he won. The incentive duly worked. Molineaux continued to fight as a free man and eventually sailed to England to seek his fortune. On arrival he met up with Richmond, who agreed to become his trainer.

After two brutal victories over highly rated English fighters, one of whom was a protégé of Cribb, Molineaux issued a challenge to the champion himself. In 1810 the pair met in freezing conditions at Copthall Common, London. For the early part of the fight the challenger had the upper hand. However, when Cribb seemed to be on the brink of defeat, his supporters rushed the ring and in the ensuing mêlée Molineaux injured his hand. When the fight resumed Cribb managed to assert his dominance; Molineaux eventually

John Heenan knocks an unidentified opponent to the ground. Heenan was known as the "Benicia Boy" for his hometown in California.

The English bare knuckle champion Tom Sayers weighed little more than 68kg (150lb), and usually had to fight men who were far larger than him. However, he still managed to win the English heavyweight title.

TOM SAYERS, CHAMPION OF ENGLAND.
Born at Pimlico, near Brighton, England, in 1826, Height 5 feet 8 inches, Fighting Weight, 150 lbs.

quit in the 33rd round. A rematch proved less controversial, as Cribb beat the challenger in less than 20 minutes.

In 1838 the sport changed, with the introduction of a new set of regulations – The London Prize Ring Rules, which replaced Broughton's Rules. The new regulations stipulated the size and shape of the ring – a square of 7.3 x 7.3m (24 x 24ft) – and stated that a mark, known as a scratch, should be made in its centre. When a man was knocked down, the round would end and there would be a 30-second break, at the end of which both fighters would have eight seconds to "come up to scratch". If either fighter failed to do so, he would lose.

Further rules banned tactics such as head butting, eye gouging and hitting below the belt, and governed the conduct of seconds.

While the champion prize fighters of England had enjoyed celebrity status, in the United States the sport had been conducted on a far more low-key basis; fights took place regularly in the early nineteenth century, but fighters were not the household names they were across the Atlantic. This state of affairs changed in 1849, with a match between James "Yankee" Sullivan and Tom Hyer. The contest had considerable political overtones. Sullivan was an Irish immigrant while Hyer was a native-born American and the contest took place at a time when there was considerable tension between the two sections of society.

Prize fighting was still illegal in the United States, so the event had to be staged at a discreet venue. Eventually, it was decided that the fight should be held on Poole's Island in Chesapeake Bay, but when the fighters set sail for the venue, they were pursued by law enforcement officials. Eventually, the combatants settled for a makeshift arena at Still Pond Heights in Maryland. There, after 16 rounds of fighting, Hyer proved

Workmen prepare to build the ring for the fight between John L. Sullivan and Jake Kilrain. The contest took place at a secret location in Mississippi in 1889.

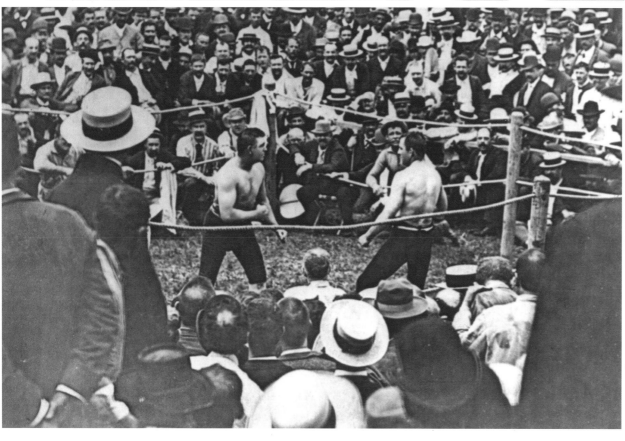

John L. Sullivan (left) prepares to strike Jake Kilrain during their contest in 1889, the last great fight of the bare knuckle era. Sullivan eventually emerged the victor.

victorious, claiming both an immense $10,000 prize and the title "champion of America".

The American boxing crown eventually passed into the hands of John C. Heenan, a big Irish-American from San Francisco. Because there were no obvious American claimants to the crown, Heenan issued a challenge to the English champion, Tom Sayers. Sayers' acceptance of the challenge set the scene for the first ever world heavyweight title fight.

Prize fighting was still technically illegal in England. However, the support of influential aristocrats had always kept the police away from major fights, and, on 17 April 1860, a conspicuously large crowd of supporters (including the novelist Charles Dickens)

made their way from London to Farnborough to watch Sayers and Heenan contest the title. At 69kg (152lb), the Englishman was over 18kg (40lb) the lighter man, and was eventually worn down, but when Heenan used the dubious tactic of driving Sayers' throat against the top rope, the crowd rioted. When the referee re-established order, a draw was declared. Sayers retired shortly afterwards, leaving Heenan as the sport's first world champion.

The popularity of prize fighting was such that many enthusiasts began to compete on an amateur basis. In 1867 John Graham Chambers, the founder of the Amateur Athletic Club, devised a set of rules to govern the contests. Chambers published the rules under the

The seconds enter the ring after a knockdown in the bare knuckle fight between John L. Sullivan and Jake Kilrain. The pair fought for 75 rounds.

sponsorship of a college friend, Sir John Sholto Douglas, the Marquess of Queensbury. This new code did much to change the brutal business of prize fighting into the sport of boxing that we know today. Key changes included the introduction of set three-minute rounds, with a one-minute break after each, and the banning of wrestling holds and throws. The clearest change between the old and new eras was a very visual one; under the new code, fighters wore gloves.

The publishing of the Marquess of Queensbury Rules did not mark the end of the bare knuckle age, merely the beginning of its end. For almost three decades, the sports of gloved boxing and bare knuckle fighting existed side by side, with most fighters competing under both codes.

The last great bare knuckle champion was also the first to defend his championship with gloves. Known as the "Boston Strong Boy", John L. Sullivan became a popular hero throughout the United States in the 1880s, renowned both for his aggressive style in the ring and drink-sodden adventures outside it. Sullivan was

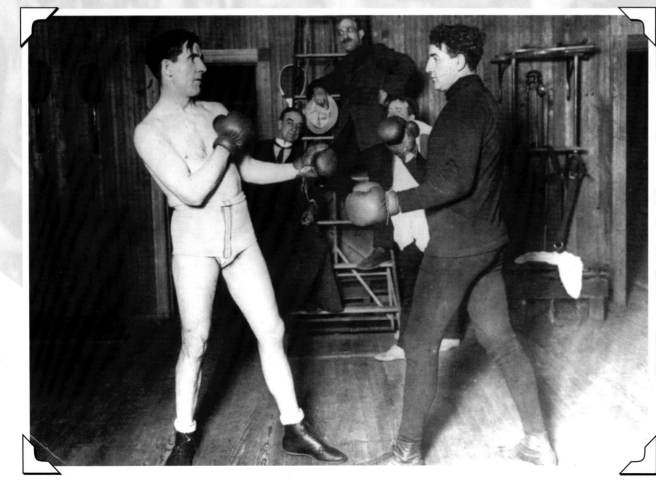

A poster showing newly crowned "champion of the world" boxer James J. Corbett, meeting with political leaders and other dignitaries from several European countries. Corbett is shown shaking hands with William E. Gladstone, Prime Minister of England. Other leaders in attendance are Queen Victoria of Great Britain, King Léopold II of Belgium, Kaiser Wilhelm II of Prussia, President Emile Loubet of France, King Umberto I of Italy, Emperor Franz Joseph I of Austria, Emperor Alexander III of Russia and Sultan Abdülhamid II, of the Turks. Across the top of the poster are emblems of several European countries.

"Gentleman" Jim Corbett (left) poses during a workout at a gym. Corbett defeated John L. Sullivan to become the first champion of the gloved era.

generally recognized as American champion when he knocked out Paddy Ryan in a bare knuckle fight in Mississippi in 1882. He then toured the United States, taking on all comers under the Marquess of Queensbury Rules, and remaining unbeaten throughout.

The last great bare knuckle match took place in 1889, when the seemingly invincible Sullivan took on Jake Kilrain in Richburg, Mississippi, a venue that was kept secret until shortly before the fight. The contest took two hours and 16 minutes, and when Kilrain's cornermen refused to let him come up to scratch for the 76th round,

the bare knuckle era unofficially came to an end.

Sullivan's next serious contest did not come until 7 September 1892, when he fought "Gentleman" Jim Corbett under Queensbury Rules. Sullivan had spent the intervening three years acting in plays and drinking heavily, and stepped into the ring badly out of shape. Corbett's skill and speed proved too much for the title holder, who was knocked out in the 21st round. The world had a new champion, the first to win his title with gloves, and the first in a succession of great fighters whose exploits would be heralded across the world.

Jim Corbett (centre) enjoys the opening game of the 1913 World Series. By this time, Corbett had retired from the ring, having lost the world title to James Jeffries 10 years earlier.

Jack Johnson

Jack Johnson was the first black fighter to win the heavyweight championship of the world. He lived in a period when racism was rife, and his battles against prejudice defined both his career in the ring and his life outside it. Johnson was born on 31 March 1878 in Galveston, Texas, where he grew up in considerable poverty. He worked from early childhood to help support his family, both on the docks of Galveston and further afield. It was on his travels in search for work that he first discovered his talent for boxing: an employer had a stock of gloves in his shop and taught him the basics of the art. Johnson had his first semi-official fight in the summer of 1895 when he fought a fellow dock worker, John Lee, on the beach at Galveston. Johnson won and claimed his first professional purse: $1.50.

Over the course of the next few years, Johnson travelled across the country working as a sparring partner and – increasingly – taking part in contests in his own right. During this period, boxing was partially segregated. Mixed-race bouts did occur, but many white boxers "drew the colour line", refusing to share the ring with black fighters, and for this reason most of Johnson's opponents were fellow African-Americans. Johnson's string of victories in these contests earned him a fight against "Denver" Ed Martin for the coloured heavyweight championship of the world, a contest that Johnson won with a decision victory after 20 rounds.

When Johnson defeated Martin in 1903, the world heavyweight champion was the brutal James Jeffries. Jeffries was seen as unbeatable by many boxing fans. One observer who did not agree with this point of view was Johnson, who was confident that he could beat the champion. For the time being he would not get the chance to prove his theory; even though he had fought several African-Americans in his early career, Jeffries was adamant that he would never allow a black challenger to fight him for his title.

Jack Johnson is photographed in a relaxed pose in March 1915, shortly before his world title fight with Jess Willard. Johnson was in the seventh year of his reign as champion of the world.

James Jeffries won the world heavyweight title in 1899, and held it until his retirement in 1905. He was lured out of retirement to fight Jack Johnson.

The Canadian Tommy Burns became world champion after the retirement of James Jeffries. He was pursued around the world by Jack Johnson. The pair eventually fought in Sydney, Australia, in 1908.

The situation changed in May 1905 when Jeffries retired from the ring. The title eventually fell into the hands of the Canadian fighter Tommy Burns. After he won the title in 1906, Burns declared that he would be prepared to face any fighter "without regard to colour, size, or nativity". In contrast to Jeffries, he wanted to be "the champion of the world, not the white or the Canadian or any other limited degree of champion". In reality, however, Burns preferred to avoid the top African-American fighters of the day, who included not only Johnson, but the very dangerous Sam Langford.

When Burns embarked on a world tour, taking on challengers in England, Ireland and France, Johnson followed, taunting the champion for his refusal to face

him. By this point, Johnson was widely regarded as the most deserving challenger for Burns's crown, and criticism of the champion was mounting. Eventually, Burns agreed to fight Johnson in Sydney, Australia. It took a $30,000 purse to tempt Burns into the ring.

The fight took place on Boxing Day, 1908. Johnson stepped out in front of a hostile crowd of around 20,000 spectators, with many more locked out of the arena. The challenger knocked down the champion shortly after the opening bell and continued to outbox Burns for 14 rounds, taunting him as he did so. Eventually the fight was stopped to save the Canadian fighter from further punishment.

Johnson was now the heavyweight champion of the world, a turn of events that caused huge controversy

Stanley Ketchel, the "Michigan Wildcat", fought a controversial fight with Jack Johnson in 1909. It was alleged that although the contest was supposed to be fixed, Ketchel reneged on the deal.

Sam Langford was one of the greatest heavyweights of the early twentieth century. He lost on points to Jack Johnson in 1906, but was never given a rematch once Johnson had become champion.

back in the United States. The world heavyweight title was seen as the ultimate prize in sport, and the fact that it was now held by an African-American provoked a fierce racist backlash. In particular, there were widespread calls for James Jeffries to come out of retirement and reclaim the title for the white race.

Initially, Jeffries declined to answer the call to return to the ring, and in the meantime Johnson fought a series of white challengers. The most notable of them was the middleweight champion Stanley Ketchel, known as the "Michigan Wildcat". Ketchel had a reputation as a ferocious puncher, but was far smaller than Johnson. In the build-up to the fight, the promoters used farcical

JOHNSON JEFFRIES

By the time that Jack Johnson and James Jeffries descended on Reno towards the end of June 1910, the Nevada town had temporarily become the centre of the sporting world. More than 300 reporters had set up camp there, and as the fight approached, thousands of fans joined them, cramming into the few available guesthouses in order to witness the so-called "Battle of the Century".

In the months leading up to the contest, newspapers had provided the public with constant updates on the state of each fighter's preparations, and the exaggerated reports of Jeffries' condition led to him entering the fight as the clear favourite. However, once the contest began, it became clear that Jeffries was no longer the fighter he once had been. Johnson controlled the fight from the outset, smothering Jeffries' attacks in the early rounds before upping the pace to inflict considerable damage on the older man. By the 11th round it was clear that Jeffries was exhausted. Finally, in the 15th, Johnson knocked him down, the first time he had experienced such a fate in his career. A second and a third knockdown followed quickly afterwards; Jeffries' corner had no option other than to throw in the towel. Jeffries later commented: "I could never have whipped Jack Johnson at my best. I couldn't have reached him in a thousand years."

While the pro-Jeffries crowd at Reno filed out of the stadium in stunned disappointment, African-American neighbourhoods erupted in joy across the country. In Chicago, a huge crowd gathered outside the house of Johnson's mother. She had followed the fight at a nearby theatre, where an announcer had read reports of each round as it ended. A local reporter recorded her thoughts at her son's victory: "There were 80 million people against him today, but he beat them all. If his father had only lived to see it! It is certainly grand to be the mother of a real hero."

There was a darker side to the fight's aftermath, however. The celebrations in African-American neighbourhoods prompted a racist backlash with lynchings reported across the country.

Jack Johnson (right) battles James Jeffries in the Reno sun. Denting the hopes of many in the crowd, Johnson outclassed the former champion. He won in the 15th round.

Jack Johnson is pictured at the wheel of one of his many automobiles. Johnson developed a passion for motor racing, and his tendency to drive at speed eventually cost him his life.

Jack Johnson poses in formal attire. Johnson always paid great attention to his personal appearance, and spent much of his ring earnings on clothes.

methods to disguise the disparity in size between the two men. For one publicity photograph, the challenger was forced to wear specially made high-heeled cowboy boots and a padded overcoat. Even so, Johnson towered over Ketchel.

The fight itself, which took place in California on 16 October 1909, proved to be highly controversial. According to Johnson, a deal had been made beforehand whereby he promised to go easy on his smaller opponent, while still doing enough to win the fight. The contest followed the pre-arranged plan for 11 rounds. In the 12th, however, Ketchel landed an

overhand right that brought Johnson to the canvas. Aware that he may have been double-crossed, the champion immediately got to his feet and knocked Ketchel unconscious.

Johnson's victory only increased the clamour for Jeffries to come out of retirement, and it was not long before the former champion gave in to public demand. On 29 October 1909, the two fighters met face to face in order to make arrangements for the contest. Eventually, it was decided that they would fight on 4 July 1910. The intervening period gave the out-of-shape Jeffries time to get back to fighting condition. It also gave the

contest's promoters an opportunity to build up interest for the fight. Predictably, the fight would be publicized as a contest for ethnic supremacy, with each man carrying the hopes of his race on his shoulders.

Johnson's victory on 4 July turned him into a hate figure for many Americans. The fact that Johnson had defeated countless white challengers was enough to earn him considerable enmity. However, the feeling was exacerbated by resentment at the boxer's ostentatious behaviour. Ever since the beginning of his career, Johnson had celebrated his wins in style. Prize money was spent quickly. Alcohol flowed freely at the parties

Jack Johnson is pictured with his arms around his mother and his wife Hattie McClay at Christmas, 1909. Johnson's numerous relationships with white women made him the target of racial hatred.

that followed his wins, and much of the money that was left over was spent on his own personal appearance. Johnson's suits were tailor-made from the finest cloth, and often decorated with diamond-encrusted jewellery. The boxer also developed a fondness for expensive automobiles, which he drove with little attention to speed limits.

But it was another aspect of Johnson's behaviour that would prove his undoing. At a time when mixed-race relationships were taboo, Johnson conducted a string of affairs with white women, who were inevitably introduced to the press simply as Mrs Johnson whether they were actually his legal wife or not. Public anger reached fever pitch when Johnson embarked on a relationship with Etta Duryea, a married woman and wealthy socialite. Following her divorce, the pair married in January 1911, but the relationship was short-lived. Duryea suffered from mental illness and committed suicide in September of that year. Some blamed Johnson, believing her mental condition had

Jack Johnson is pictured with his wife Lucille. Lucille's family was bitterly opposed to the relationship. Her mother instigated a campaign against the boxer that eventually led to his imprisonment.

Jack and Lucille Johnson board a ship during the boxer's exile from the United States. The Johnsons spent much of this period in Europe, where Jack became a considerable celebrity.

Known as the "Pittsburgh Dentist" because of his original hometown profession, Frank Moran was a tough heavyweight who had learned to fight in the navy. He fought Jack Johnson for the world title in 1914, but lost on points.

Jess Willard is photographed in 1915, shortly before his title fight with Jack Johnson. Although he was not a particularly skilful boxer, Willard's huge size made him a difficult opponent.

been made worse by his womanizing. The scandal was heightened by the fact that by the end of the year, Johnson had married again, to another white woman, Lucille Cameron.

This relationship would prove costly. Cameron's mother claimed that Johnson had kidnapped her daughter, which gave the authorities an excuse to pursue him. When the Cameron case collapsed, the Bureau of Investigation (the forerunner of the FBI) changed tack, investigating Johnson's earlier relationship with the white prostitute Belle Schreiber. On 4 June 1912, Johnson was convicted under the Mann Act for transporting a woman across state lines for immoral purposes. However, while he was waiting for his appeal to be heard, Johnson fled the country, first to Canada and then to France.

Johnson would remain in exile for eight years. He continued to lead the extravagant lifestyle that he had followed at home, but earning opportunities were

Jess Willard towers over Jack Johnson after knocking him out in the 26th round of their fight in Havana, Cuba. The fact that Johnson appears to be shielding his eyes from the sun led to the mistaken rumour that the knockout was faked.

becoming limited. Johnson defended his heavyweight title twice while in France. The first was a lacklustre draw against his namesake Jim Johnson, while the second was a 20-round points win over Frank Moran, a fight that Johnson had unsuccessfully tried to fix beforehand. The outbreak of the First World War then forced Johnson to move to London, where the promoter Jack Curley had a proposition for him: a fight against the giant cowboy, Jess Willard. Johnson eagerly agreed.

Johnson's fight against Willard took place on 5 April 1915 in Havana, Cuba. While Willard was a crude and inexperienced fighter, his size alone made him extremely dangerous. He stood over 1.98m (6ft 6in) tall and weighed almost 109kg (240lb). The difference in size was not the only factor that would be in Willard's favour; the fight was scheduled for 45 rounds in the intense midday Havana heat, and the conditions favoured the younger challenger. While Johnson controlled the early part of the contest, he was unable to inflict serious damage on his opponent, who became more dominant as the fight wore on. Finally, in the 26th round an overhand right from Willard knocked Johnson out, ending his reign as champion of the world.

After the fight, Johnson returned to Europe, where he eked out a living at boxing exhibitions, as well as pursuing an unlikely career as a bullfighter. Eventually, though, he returned to the United States. On 20 July 1920, Johnson handed himself over to the authorities in a high-profile ceremony. He went on to serve a one-year jail sentence.

After his release in July 1921, Johnson continued to box, but against increasingly insignificant opposition and his vociferous demands for a chance to fight once again for the world championship were ignored. His last fight did not come until 1938, by which time he was 60 years old.

Johnson's death would come after one final brush with racism. In 1946 he stopped to eat at a roadside diner in North Carolina, but was told he could only eat in the back of the restaurant. An angry Johnson sped off into the night, only to lose control of his car and crash into a telephone pole. He died in hospital hours later.

Mourners file past the coffin of Jack Johnson at a memorial service held in June, 1946. Johnson had died in an automobile accident in Raleigh, North Carolina.

Jack Dempsey

One of the United States' earliest sports stars, Jack Dempsey was a brutal and charismatic boxer whose fights inspired huge levels of excitement. He once drew more than 120,000 spectators to a single contest. William Harrison Dempsey was born in Manassa, Colorado, on 24 June 1895, the ninth of 13 children. He grew up in poverty, leaving home at 16 to travel the country on freight trains in search of work. During this period he worked at everything from crop picking to mining, but supplemented his earnings by fighting in saloons for hatfuls of change. Dempsey would walk into bars and issue an open challenge to the patrons, claiming that he could "lick any son of a bitch in the house". He was usually true to his word, and quickly built up a reputation as an aggressive knockout artist.

In addition to these impromptu bar brawls, Dempsey also took part in more conventional contests. In his early fights around the mining towns of Colorado, Dempsey competed under the name "Kid Blackie". However, he eventually assumed the name that he is known by today; he called himself "Jack" after an earlier Irish boxer Jack "Nonpareil" Dempsey, who had fought in the late nineteenth century. The younger Jack Dempsey also picked up another name that was to stay with him to his grave: the "Manassa Mauler", a soubriquet bestowed on him by the writer Damon Runyon during a trip to New York.

In 1917, when the United States entered the First World War, Dempsey opted to remain in civilian life, a choice that would later see him labelled a draft dodger. He put the war years to good use, however, putting together a string of victories that established his name as an exciting up-and-coming heavyweight. Dempsey's popularity was the result largely of his aggressive, all-action style. He pursued his opponents relentlessly around the ring throwing a barrage of hooks from a crouched stance. Standing 1.85m (6ft 1in) tall and

This photograph of Jack Dempsey was taken in 1920, the year after he won the heavyweight championship of the world. Known as the "Manassa Mauler", Dempsey was one of the most celebrated sporting figures of his era.

The "Battling Levinsky", originally known as Barney Williams, had already beaten more than 140 men by the time he faced Jack Dempsey in November 1918. Dempsey's victory proved that he was a force to be reckoned with.

Jack Dempsey is pictured with his manager Jack Kearns in 1923. Kearns was hugely adept at publicizing his fighter, and helped make his 1921 fight with Georges Carpentier a major event.

connections were important. Fortunately for Dempsey, in 1917 he had met Jack "Doc" Kearns, a former fighter who had gravitated towards management. Accounts of how they met vary. Kearns, always keen to build up a myth, claimed that the pair had met when Dempsey helped him out in a bar fight. The truth may have been more prosaic; it is likely that Kearns simply saw Dempsey fight and realized that he could make a large amount of money by promoting the young crowd-pleaser. Kearns' ambitions were realized when Dempsey met Jess Willard for the heavyweight championship of the world on 4 July 1919.

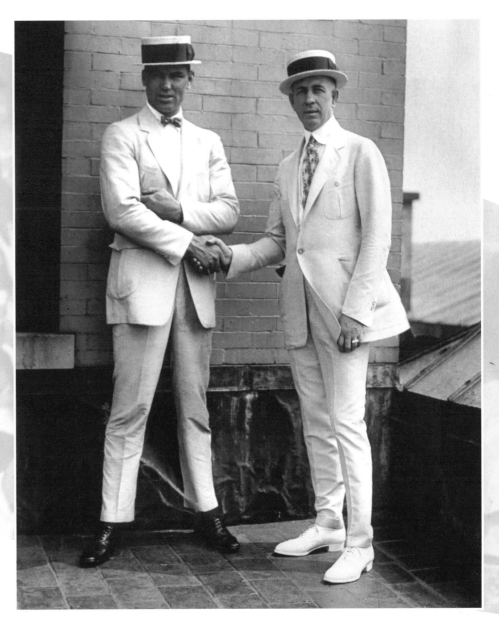

weighing around 86kg (190lb), Dempsey was not particularly big for a heavyweight (particularly by modern standards) but made up for his comparative lack of stature by his uncompromising nature.

It was in 1918 that Dempsey began to establish himself as a genuine contender for the heavyweight crown. Dempsey fought 21 times over the course of the year, finishing with a record of 19 wins, one draw and one loss. Twelve of the wins came by way of first-round knockout. Among Dempsey's victims were several fighters with big reputations. The "Battling Levinsky", whom Dempsey fought on 6 November 1918, was a veteran of over 200 contests and the current light heavyweight champion of the world. Up until this point he had never been knocked out, but this record was brought to a halt by Dempsey, who knocked his opponent out in the third round.

Ring exploits alone weren't enough to earn Dempsey a shot at the world title. As in any era of boxing,

DEMPSEY

WILLARD

In 1919 the world heavyweight title was held by Jess Willard. A 1.98m (6ft 6in) cowboy, Willard had not boxed until the age of 29, but had turned to the ring in desperation after being swindled by business partners. In 1915 he had been given the chance to fight Jack Johnson, an opportunity that he unexpectedly took advantage of when he knocked the heavyweight champion out in the 26th round.

To many observers, Dempsey went into the fight against Willard as a clear underdog. Willard was over 25kg (55lb) heavier than the challenger and 13cm (5in) taller. However, in other respects, Dempsey came to the contest with significant advantages. The previous two years had seen Dempsey constantly active as a fighter – at times he had three or four contests a month. Willard meanwhile had fought only twice since his victory over Johnson in Havana. The former cowboy had only entered the boxing business reluctantly, and, once he became champion, showed little enthusiasm for defending his title. Nevertheless, he did not lack for belief in his own abilities, saying, "There isn't a man living who

Jack Dempsey (right) drives Jess Willard into a corner during their world title fight in July, 1919. Although he was by far the smaller man, Dempsey easily overpowered his opponent.

can hurt me, no matter where he hits me or how often he lands." This confidence would prove to be very much misplaced.

The two fighters met at Bay View Park Arena, Toledo, Ohio, in front of a huge crowd. The first round would go down as one of the most ferocious in heavyweight title history. After an initial period in which the two fighters cautiously circled one another, Dempsey closed the distance and caught Willard with a flurry of hooks, knocking the taller man to the canvas. Willard got to his feet only to be caught with a second barrage. The process was repeated throughout the round. At this point in boxing history, fighters did not have to return to a neutral corner after knocking an opponent down. Dempsey took advantage of this loophole, repeatedly hovering over Willard as he regained his feet and then unleashing a hook the first moment it was legal. By the time the bell sounded for the end of the first round, the champion had been knocked down seven times in total.

Despite the terrible beating he had taken, Willard returned after the bell, managing to survive the second and third rounds despite enduring considerable further punishment. At the end of the third,

Jack Dempsey (left) poses in the gym with fight promoter George "Tex" Rickard. Rickard was involved in many of the most high-profile fights of the early twentieth century.

Jack Dempsey (left) prepares to strike Jess Willard as soon as he rises. Willard was knocked down repeatedly during their encounter.

however, he quit on his stool. Dempsey was the new heavyweight champion of the world.

The defeat took a terrible toll on Willard. It left him with four fractured ribs, a broken jaw and six fewer teeth. He would fight only twice more. For Dempsey, the contest would make him one of the most recognizable sportsmen in America. However, financial reward would have to wait. Unbeknown to Dempsey, his manager Kearns had wagered the fighter's entire purse on a first-round knockout. Dempsey would make no money from his greatest triumph.

Dempsey's first defence of his title came just over a year later. His opponent was Billy Miske, the "St. Paul Thunderbolt". Miske was known as a tough and durable boxer and had fought Dempsey twice before, one contest ending in a win for Dempsey and another in a draw. However, Miske was not the fighter he had once been: he had recently been diagnosed with a serious kidney disease and was only fighting out of financial desperation. The fight ended with a KO win for Dempsey in the third round.

Dempsey's second fight in 1920 came against another former opponent, Bill Brennan, whom Dempsey had stopped in six rounds in 1918. On that occasion Dempsey had won easily, knocking Brennan down four times in a single round. The second fight was more closely contested. Brennan hurt the champion early on, but Dempsey eventually wore his opponent down before stopping him in the 12th.

By 1921 Dempsey had become an unpopular figure with the American public at large, mainly because of the popular belief that he was a draft dodger. At the time of the First World War, Dempsey escaped service because he claimed that he had to support his family in Colorado. However, in divorce proceedings Dempsey's wife Maxine Cates stated that she in fact supported him. The fact that Cates was a prostitute heightened the scandal. Fortunately for Dempsey, someone was on hand to turn the situation to his advantage. The boxing promoter Tex Rickard had developed a very close relationship with Dempsey's manager Jack Kearns, and devised a strategy for capitalizing on Dempsey's poor public image.

One of the most obvious challengers for Dempsey's crown was the charismatic Frenchman Georges Carpentier, who had begun fighting as a flyweight while still a teenager and had gradually risen up through the

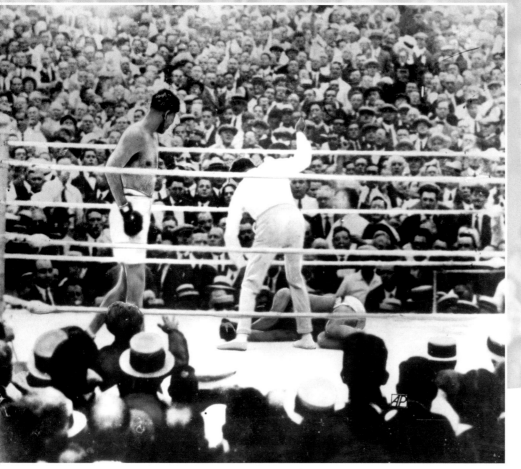

Jack Demspey watches the referee begin his count over the prostrate body of Georges Carpentier. Carpentier lost their 1921 encounter in the fourth round.

Jack Dempsey's fight with Georges Carpentier was watched by more than 80,000 spectators. The huge attendance was at least partially the result of the pre-fight publicity generated by "Tex" Rickard.

weight categories. In October 1920 he had defeated the "Battling Levinsky" to win the world light heavyweight championship. There was a huge difference in fighting style between the skilful boxer Carpentier and the rugged brawler Dempsey. Another contrast between the two men lay in their respective war records. Unlike Dempsey, Carpentier had served his country with distinction, winning the War Cross and the Military Medal for bravery.

In the run-up to the fight, Rickard used the media to turn the fight into an epic contest between good and evil, an approach that reaped huge financial rewards at the box office. When the two fighters stepped out to meet each other in Jersey City on 2 July 1921, they did so in front of an immense crowd of 80,183 who between them paid almost $1.8 million for the privilege, a record for a boxing match. The fight made history in another sense as well, being the first to be broadcast nationally on radio. As a contest, however, the fight proved to be

Tommy Gibbons fought Jack Dempsey in Shelby, Montana, in July, 1923. Gibbons survived the full 15 rounds, but lost the decision.

Jack Dempsey looks down at the defeated Luis Angel Firpo. Their fight was one of the most eventful heavyweight title fights in history, with 11 knockdowns in just two rounds.

less memorable. Although Carpentier managed to rock the champion in the second round, Dempsey's greater weight and strength soon began to tell and he knocked the Frenchman out in the fourth.

After the Carpentier match, Dempsey increasingly began to turn his back on the world of boxing to enjoy the celebrity lifestyle that his ring exploits had earned him. His next non-exhibition fight did not come for another two years, a fairly routine points victory over Tommy Gibbons. The fight was mainly notable for practically bankrupting Shelby, Montana, the town that hosted it.

Gene Tunney (left) attacks Jack Dempsey during the first of the pair's two encounters. The fight, held in September 1926, was contested in front of a record 120,557 people.

Jack Dempsey poses with his wife, the actress Estelle Taylor. Thanks to his wife's connections, Dempsey increasingly began to mix in Hollywood circles.

The Gibbons fight was followed closely by a contest against the giant Argentinian Luis Angel Firpo, which proved to be far more eventful than its immediate predecessor. At first the contest seemed a carbon copy of Dempsey's fight against Willard, as Dempsey bullied the larger challenger around the ring. Firpo was knocked down several times in the first round, but recovered to throw a punch that lifted Dempsey clean out of the ring. Dempsey only beat the count thanks to the help of some ringside reporters who pushed him back through the ropes. However, the champion survived the round and reasserted his dominance in the second, knocking out his challenger to keep his title.

After the Firpo fight, Dempsey did not defend his title for three years, preferring the company of Hollywood stars to sparring partners. He moved to Los Angeles and married the actress Estelle Taylor, confining his ring appearances to numerous exhibition bouts. Eventually, however, public opinion forced him back in the ring.

By 1926 the leading contender for Dempsey's title was Gene Tunney, the "Fighting Marine". Like Carpentier, Tunney was a contrast to Dempsey not just in fighting style but also in personality. Articulate and clean-living, he liked to amuse bystanders with quotations from Shakespeare. Behind the cultivated exterior, however, lay an extremely tough and talented boxer who had fought 81 times as a professional and been defeated only once.

Dempsey and Tunney met in pouring rain at the Sesquicentennial Stadium in Philadelphia on 23 September 1926. The crowd was a new record for a boxing match – 120,557. The champion was a heavy favourite, yet it soon became clear that three years of inactivity had taken their toll. Dempsey was unable to impose his aggressive style on his opponent as the challenger skilfully outboxed him. After 10 rounds Tunney was awarded a unanimous decision. The world had a new heavyweight boxing champion.

Before he could attempt to reclaim his title, Dempsey first had to fight an elimination contest against a tough Boston fighter by the name of Jack Sharkey. For six rounds Sharkey more than held his own against the former champion, forcing a desperate Dempsey to fight dirty. The fight came to an end in the seventh after a low blow by Dempsey caused Sharkey to look to the referee in protest. Taking advantage of Sharkey's lack of concentration, Dempsey threw a hook that knocked his opponent out.

The rematch against Tunney came on 22 September 1927. Before the fight Dempsey's camp requested that the fight should be contested under a new rule that insisted that a fighter must retire to a neutral corner after knocking his opponent down, a decision that would have a major bearing on the fight's outcome. After being outboxed for six rounds, Dempsey landed a

Gene Tunney ties Dempsey up in their 1926 encounter. Dempsey looked to be suffering from ring rust, and lost a decision to his challenger.

hard punch in the seventh that left Tunney on the canvas. However, Dempsey hovered over his opponent rather than retiring to his corner. The referee refused to start the count until Dempsey did so, giving Tunney an extra five seconds to recover. He eventually got up, recovered and boxed out the remaining five rounds to claim a points victory.

The "Fight of the Long Count" split boxing fans. Supporters of Dempsey claimed that if the referee had begun his count immediately, Dempsey would have reclaimed his title. Tunney, however, later said that he was simply waiting for the count of "nine" to rise and would have got up earlier if he had needed to.

Jack Dempsey knocks Gene Tunney to the canvas in their much anticipated rematch, held in September, 1927 at Soldier Field, Chicago.

Whatever the truth, the match proved to be Dempsey's final contest.

Dempsey spent a long retirement enjoying the fruits of the celebrity that his fights had earned; between 1935 and 1974 he was the conspicuous proprietor of Jack Dempsey's Broadway Restaurant in New York. He died on 31 May 1983, aged 87.

Referee Dave Barry counts over a stricken Gene Tunney, during his rematch with Jack Dempsey. The controversy of the "long count" would haunt Barry for the rest of his life.

Jack Dempsey walks past his fabled restaurant in New York. The diner was a regular haunt of Dempsey during his retirement.

Joe Louis

Even if he were to be evaluated purely on his abilities as a boxer, Joe Louis would be seen as one of the greatest fighters in the history of the sport. The so-called "Brown Bomber" defended the world heavyweight championship 25 times, more than anyone either before or since. However, his victory over the German Max Schmeling in 1938 elevated him to a symbolic status that transcended the sport, an emblem of American opposition to the Nazi regime of Adolf Hitler.

Joe Louis Barrow was born on 13 May 1914 in Lafayette, Alabama, and grew up in considerable poverty. His father, a sharecropper, was committed to a mental hospital when Louis was only two years old and his mother supported the family by washing clothes before moving in with a local widower, Pat Brooks. In 1926 the family travelled north to live in Detroit, a move that was prompted partly by the employment opportunities offered by the city's automobile industry and partly by the racism prevalent in the south; earlier that year the family had encountered a Ku Klux Klan lynch mob late at night and had only narrowly escaped being killed.

Louis began boxing while still at school, playing truant to train at the Brewster Recreation Center. Dropping his surname and fighting simply under the name "Joe Louis", he made his debut against the experienced light heavyweight Johnny Miller in 1932. Louis's performance offered little hint of what was to come; he was knocked down seven times on the way to a defeat. However, he refined his skills quickly and by 1934 he had an amateur record of 50 wins and only four defeats.

Louis turned professional the same year. He was to be helped by a shrewd and streetwise management team. John Roxborough and Julian Black were both involved in running numbers games, a form of gambling that was popular in poor African-American neighbourhoods.

The "Brown Bomber," otherwise known as Joe Louis, poses in January, 1937, when he was just 22. By the end of the year, he would be heavyweight champion of the world.

punch from Louis knocked Carnera to the canvas. The Italian got up at the count of four only to be knocked down for a second time. A third fall shortly afterwards left the referee with little choice but to end the bout.

After the Carnera fight, momentum built for Louis to get a shot at the title. A first-round win over King Levinsky was followed by a shot at a second former champion, the charismatic, wisecracking Max Baer. Baer had won the title by defeating Carnera, and then promptly lost it in his first title defence against the journeyman Jim Braddock. Baer was an unpredictable fighter, immensely talented, but no fan of disciplined training regimes. Louis had little difficulty dispatching his big-hitting but wild opponent inside four rounds. When Louis knocked him down for the third time, Baer made no attempt to rise to his feet. He later remarked: "When I get executed, people are going to have to pay more than $25 a seat to watch it."

Louis won two more fights in quick succession before meeting the fighter with whom he would always be associated, the German Max Schmeling. Schmeling was a regular presence in American rings, having fought in

The pair's expertise was in making money, not boxing, so they employed a former lightweight boxer named Jack Blackburn to train Louis. Together the trio would mastermind Louis's rise to the top.

Louis's ascent up the professional ranks was just as rapid as his amateur rise. His first fight came on 4 July 1934 and ended in spectacular fashion when Louis knocked his opponent, Jack Kracken, through the ropes and into the lap of the chairman of the Illinois Athletic Commission. Another 17 victories came in quick succession, creating a demand for Louis to face a name opponent. That opponent was to be Primo Carnera, a giant Italian who had held the world heavyweight title between 1933 and 1934. A former circus strongman and wrestler, Carnera was held in low regard by boxing aficionados, who derided him for his clumsy style and history of fixed fights. However, at 1.98m (6ft 6in) tall and 118kg (260lb), his sheer size and strength had caused problems for many more talented heavyweights.

The fight, which took place in New York on 25 June 1935, proved to any doubters that Louis was capable of competing at the highest level. For the first five rounds he dominated his larger opponent, making light of the 27kg (60lb) weight difference between the two fighters. In the sixth, the destruction began. A right

Joe Louis is photographed with the team that guided him in the early part of his career. They include his trainer Jack Blackburn (second left) and his manager John Roxborough (second right).

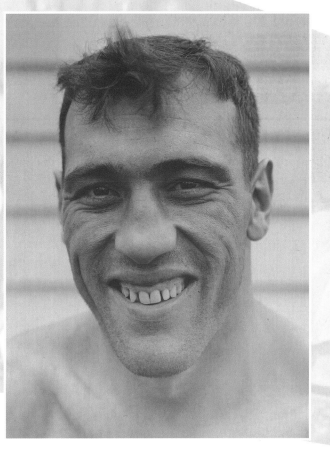

Primo Carnera smiles for the cameras shortly before his June 1935 fight with Joe Louis. Former champion Carnera was known for his huge size and limited ability.

the United States since 1928. He was the third former heavyweight champion to have faced Louis, but was not expected to pose a serious threat to the younger fighter, who was on a 23-fight winning streak. Nevertheless, Schmeling had noticed a technical weakness in the younger fighter's game, a tendency to drop his left hand after throwing a jab. This habit left Louis's chin exposed. Schmeling exploited this weakness throughout their fight, which took place on 19 June 1936. After knocking Louis down for the first time in his career, he went on to knock him out in the 12th round.

Louis's defeat did not harm his chances of getting a shot at the world championship as much as might have been expected. Louis remained active and a run of seven consecutive victories was enough to earn him a fight against Jim Braddock, who had not fought since upsetting Max Baer two years earlier. The contest marked the first time that a white fighter had given a black challenger an opportunity to win the title since

Joe Louis (left) weighs in for his fight against King Levinsky in August, 1935. It would prove to be a short night's work for Louis: he won in just two minutes and 21 seconds.

Joe Louis lands a punch to the stomach of Primo Carnera during the course of their 1935 contest. Louis won by knockout in the sixth round.

Tommy Burns had fought Jack Johnson almost 30 years previously. Aware of the hatred that Johnson had aroused in white audiences, Louis's management team had carefully controlled his public image in an attempt to make him appear the opposite of Johnson: whereas Johnson had been brash, extrovert and dismissive of his opponents, Louis was groomed to appear modest and respectful.

Louis's chance to claim the heavyweight title came on 22 June 1937, when he faced Braddock at Comiskey Park, Chicago. Pre-fight newspaper reports had centered on Louis's laid-back demeanour in training and suggested that he wasn't taking the fight seriously. A first-round knockdown courtesy of a Braddock uppercut suggested that they might be right, but Louis got up immediately and from this point onward dominated his opponent. Over the course of the subsequent rounds, Louis inflicted considerable damage, and by the end of the seventh Braddock's face was badly swollen. The end came in the eighth when

LOUIS

SCHMELING

After knocking Max Schmeling to the floor, Joe Louis heads to a neutral corner to allow referee Arthur Donovan to begin the count. Schmeling was knocked down three times in just a single round.

Joe Louis's 1938 title defence against Max Schmeling had greater political overtones than any other fight in history. The German's earlier win over Louis had been greeted by the Nazi authorities as a huge propaganda coup. A congratulatory telegram from Goebbels had told Schmeling, "Your victory is a German victory", while Nazi party newspaper reports had hailed it as proof of the superiority of the white race. In the intervening two years, the stakes had grown higher as the world became aware of the Nazi threat. Both governments began to invest heavily in the result of the contest, with President Franklin D. Roosevelt personally informing Louis of his responsibilities.

Despite a campaign by US anti-Nazi agitators to have the fight cancelled, the contest took place on 22 June at Yankee Stadium, New York. It would prove to be Louis's defining performance in the ring. Inspired by racist comments allegedly made by Schmeling to the press (later denied) and a desire to avenge his earlier loss, Louis displayed an aggression that had been absent in the first encounter. A succession of fierce combinations drove Schmeling towards the ropes where he turned his

Joe Louis lands a right hook to the ribs of Max Schmeling in the opening moments of their 1938 rematch.

A crowd in Washington DC celebrates Joe Louis's victory over Max Schmeling. The fight, pitting an American against a representative of Hitler's Nazi regime, assumed huge significance for the people of the United States.

back on the champion. The referee began to count, before waving the fight on. Schmeling went down three more times before the contest was stopped. In total, the fight had taken a mere two minutes and four seconds.

The fight transformed Louis into a national hero, but for Schmeling, its consequences were less positive. The German had always been a reluctant standard bearer of the Nazi regime, and had angered its leaders with his refusal to join the party or sack his Jewish manager Joe Jacobs. While he was winning, such indiscretions were tolerated, but now he had been defeated, he fell quickly out of favour. The boxer found himself conscripted into the paratroop regiment. He injured himself during an operation in Crete and was taken prisoner by the Allies.

After the war, Schmeling became a successful businessman, and his story became entwined with that of Louis once again. The two became friends in later life, and Schmeling helped Louis when the American boxer fell into financial difficulties. He is also believed to have contributed to the costs of Louis's funeral.

Max Schmeling (right) lands a right to the jaw of Joe Louis in the pair's first encounter in 1936. Schmeling knocked Louis out in the 12th round.

James Braddock (right) exchanges punches with Joe Louis in 1937. Louis beat the "Cinderella Man" in eight rounds to claim the world heavyweight title. It was Braddock's first defence of his crown.

Braddock was knocked down and unable to return to his feet. Louis was the champion of the world.

After three successful defences against Tommy Farr, Nathan Mann and Harry Thomas, Louis turned his attention to the one fighter who had defeated him as a professional: Max Schmeling.

After his defeat of Schmeling, Louis began a long winning streak, defending his title a further 15 times before the United States entered the Second World War on 8 December 1941. Many of the defences were routine fights against overmatched boxers, derided by sports writers as the "Bum of the Month Club", but towards the

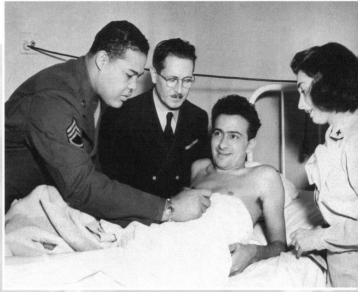

Joe Louis signs the cast of an injured serviceman during a tour of a naval hospital in March, 1945. Louis spent much of the Second World War making public appearances in an effort to boost troop morale.

end of this period, Louis fought an epic contest against one of the best fighters of his era, Billy Conn.

Like Louis, Conn was on a long victorious streak, during which he had won the world light heavyweight title before moving up to heavyweight. When the two fighters clashed on 18 June 1941, Conn was outweighed by over 11kg (25lb). However, he managed to use this discrepancy to his advantage, dancing around the champion and landing a far greater number of punches. By the end of the 12th round, Conn was clearly ahead; he only had to continue his tactics for another three rounds to claim a famous victory. Conn went for glory, however, electing to trade punches with Louis in an attempt to knock the champion out. It was a mistake he would regret for the rest of his life; one brutal barrage by Louis brought the fight to a swift conclusion.

On 10 January 1942, Louis enlisted in the US Army. Although he would not see active service, Louis would play a major role in the US propaganda effort, appearing on recruitment posters, visiting wounded soldiers in hospital and taking part in exhibition bouts. He also made two successful defences of his world heavyweight crown, against Buddy Baer and Abe Simon, donating his purses to military relief funds.

After the Second World War, Louis returned to the ring, defending his title twice more before facing

Billy Conn stumbles to the canvas after being struck by Joe Louis in the 13th round of their title fight. The knockout saved Louis: he was behind on points at the time.

"Jersey Joe" Walcott, a former sparring partner. It was clear that Louis's powers were on the wane. Walcott dominated the contest and was extremely unfortunate to emerge as the loser by way of a split decision. A rematch on 25 June 1948 provided Louis with a more clear-cut victory – he won by stoppage in the 11th round – but Walcott again caused him serious problems. Louis announced his retirement nine months afterwards. He had been champion for almost 12 years.

The champion's retirement was short lived. Over the course of his later career, he had built up huge debts, partly as the result of an extravagant lifestyle, but partly because the IRS had taxed him on the purses he donated to the army relief fund. He returned to the ring on 27 September 1950 to fight new champion Ezzard Charles, but was no match for the younger fighter, losing via unanimous decision. Undeterred by the

Like many great champions, Joe Louis ended his days in the ring with a performance that did not befit his career. Rocky Marciano (right) proved far too strong in their 1951 contest.

setback, Louis fought on, putting together a string of eight consecutive victories before taking on future champion Rocky Marciano at Madison Square Garden. During the early rounds, Louis more than held his own, but as the fight wore on, the tide turned. The former champion grew weary. Eventually, in the eighth round, Marciano knocked Louis clean through the ropes to bring an ignominious end to one of the greatest careers in boxing history.

While Louis's second retirement was longer than his first, it was no happier. He continued to be pursued by the IRS for unpaid taxes. Other creditors were equally persistent and Louis was often reliant on family and friends for financial support. Spells of drug addiction and incarceration for mental illness followed, though Louis recovered sufficiently to work as a greeter at a Las Vegas casino. He died of a heart attack in 1981.

Sugar Ray Robinson

Muhammad Ali spent much of his career proclaiming himself "the Greatest". When pressed, however, Ali would admit that the title belonged to a fighter from an earlier era: Sugar Ray Robinson. Robinson was born Walker Smith Jr on 3 May 1921. Sometime around the date of his birth, Robinson's family moved from rural Georgia to the industrial city of Detroit, a journey made by countless other African-Americans at that time. In 1932 Robinson relocated once again, this time to New York City. Robinson got his first taste of boxing on the streets, but his skills would be refined at the Salem Crescent gym on Seventh Avenue, where he trained under George Gainford.

It was Gainford who would be responsible for the young Walker Smith changing his name. When Smith turned up at his first boxing tournament, he found that he could not compete because he was not a member of the Amateur Athletic Union. Gainford got round the problem by giving him an AAU membership card belonging to another of his fighters, Ray Robinson. He would continue to fight under this name for the rest of his career. The nickname "Sugar" was added shortly afterwards, when Gainford was informed he had a sweet fighter on his hands. "Sweet as sugar," replied a nearby woman.

Robinson would go on to have a hugely successful amateur career, recording 85 wins with no defeats, with 69 of the victories coming by way of knockout. Looking to alleviate his family's poverty, he turned professional on 4 October 1940, knocking out Joe Echevarria in the second round. Robinson earned $150 for the fight, a considerable amount for a poor family.

Robinson's professional career progressed rapidly. Five more wins followed that year, largely against mediocre fighters. However, in 1941, Sugar Ray began to impose himself against a higher class of opposition. He fought 20 times in all, winning on every occasion. One of

Sugar Ray Robinson poses for the cameras in May, 1947. He had won the world welterweight championship the previous year.

his most notable victims was the current world lightweight champion Sammy Angott. Because the fight was held above the lightweight limit of 62kg (136lb), the champion's title was not on the line, but Robinson's clear victory established him as a fighter to be watched.

The following year saw a sequence of 14 straight victories, including a return win against Angott. This run also included a first contest between Robinson and the fighter who would become his most famous rival, Jake LaMotta. While Robinson won this initial meeting,

LaMotta would soon get his revenge. In February, 1943, Robinson returned to his old home city of Detroit to once again take on the fighter known as the "Bronx Bull". The contest was held at middleweight, giving LaMotta a 7kg (16lb) weight advantage. The Italian American used the difference to his advantage, knocking Robinson through the ropes on his way to a 10-round unanimous decision. A third fight took place at the same venue, just three weeks later, with Robinson proving victorious by way of a 10-round decision.

Jake LaMotta (left) knocks Sugar Ray Robinson through the ropes en route to winning their fight in February, 1943. It was Robinson's first defeat as a professional, but he would get his revenge just three weeks later.

On 27 February, the day after his second win over LaMotta, Robinson was inducted into the US Army. There he was reunited with the other great fighter of his generation, Joe Louis. The pair had first met in Detroit, where as a young child Robinson had carried local hero Louis's bag to the Brewster Recreation Center, where he trained. The two fighters' paths had crossed frequently since then, and now they embarked on a tour of military camps to raise troop morale.

Robinson's period of military service ended abruptly when he was hospitalized following a fall. He was given an honourable discharge on 3 June 1944. He had fought only three times during his time in the army, and one of these contests was essentially an act of charity. Robinson's childhood hero Henry Armstrong had fallen on hard times, and Sugar Ray agreed to fight him, even though Armstrong was no longer in a fit state to give him a reasonable contest. Robinson cruised to a decision victory, giving both himself and Armstrong a sizeable paycheck.

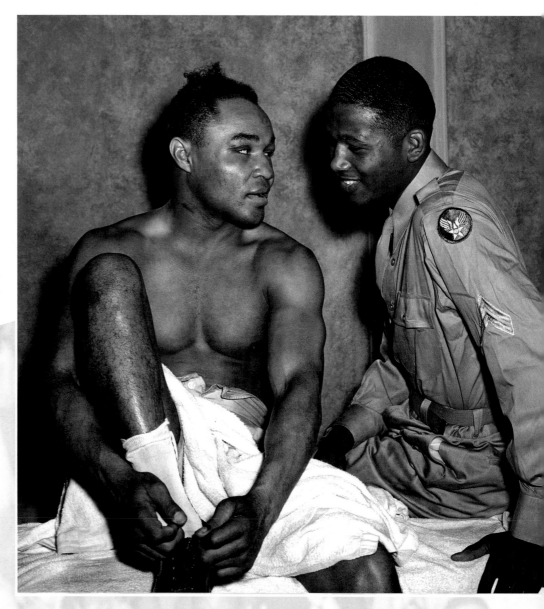

Sugar Ray Robinson (right, in army uniform) chats with former world champion Henry Armstrong a few days before their clash in August, 1943. By this point in his career, Armstrong was well past his prime.

The great Cuban welterweight Kid Gavilan was one of Sugar Ray Robinson's toughest opponents. The pair fought twice, once in 1948 and once in 1949.

Robinson's combination of speed, grace and power had made him a star, but despite his long run of success – his loss against LaMotta remained his only defeat – he had yet to fight for a world title. Sugar Ray prolonged his winning streak throughout the next two years and eventually, in December 1946, he was rewarded with a shot at the welterweight title. By the time he stepped into the ring with Tommy Bell at Madison Square Garden, New York, Robinson's record stood at 73 wins, one loss, and one draw. Bell was to become his 74th victim, but not before giving Robinson a severe test. Sugar Ray was knocked down in the early rounds, but recovered to win a unanimous 15-round decision.

A bloodied and battered Sugar Ray Robinson (right) throws a right to the jaw of Englishman Randolph Turpin during his 1951 attempt to regain the world middleweight title. Robinson eventually won in the 10th round.

ROBINSON

LAMOTTA

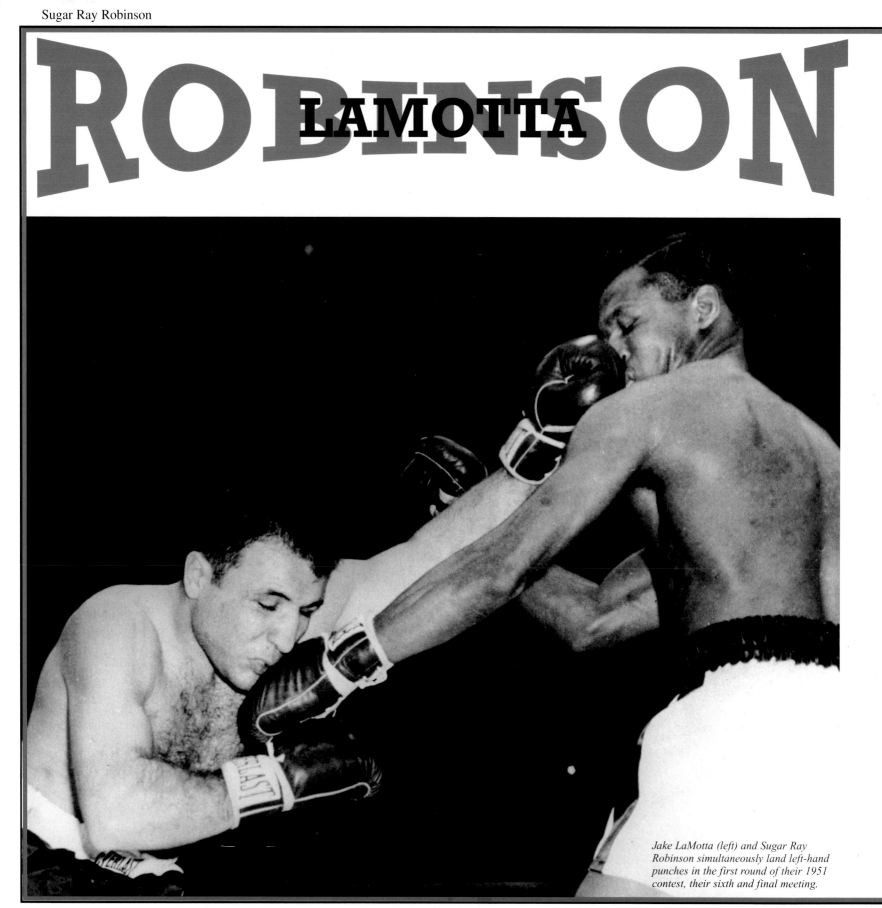

Jake LaMotta (left) and Sugar Ray Robinson simultaneously land left-hand punches in the first round of their 1951 contest, their sixth and final meeting.

Sugar Ray Robinson's second victory over Jake LaMotta in 1943 did not mark the climax of the pair's ring rivalry, but merely the halfway point. The boxers fought twice more in 1945, with Robinson emerging the victor by decision on both occasions. The second of these two contests was particularly close, with LaMotta rallying strongly in the fight's closing stages. He would put these setbacks behind him to claim the world middleweight title with a win over Marcel Cerdan. Two successful defences set up a sixth clash with Robinson.

The pair met on 14 February 1951, a date that would give the fight the title the "St. Valentine's Day Massacre". The early rounds of the fight followed the pattern of the two boxers' earlier contests, set by their contrasting styles. LaMotta came forward in a crouched stance while

A right hand from Robinson grazes the head of LaMotta. Robinson bleeds from his lip, yet it would be LaMotta who would suffer the most damage in the contest.

Sugar Ray Robinson (right) throws a right hand in the 13th and final round of the so-called "St. Valentine's Day Massacre". The punishment endured by Jake LaMotta during the course of the round forced the referee to stop the contest.

Robinson used his superior footwork to keep out of range and sting his opponent with fast jabs. As the fight wore on, however, Robinson's punches became more ferocious. By the 12th round he was hitting LaMotta at will. It was stopped in the 13th with the "Bronx Bull" still on his feet but incapable of defending himself. LaMotta later commented: "If the fight had gone another 20 seconds, Robinson would have collapsed from hitting me so much."

Although LaMotta continued to box for another three years, he never again reached the heights of his earlier career. Later, his reputation was sullied when he admitted throwing a 1947 fight with Billy Fox in return for a future title shot. The revelation led to LaMotta being ostracized in boxing circles. When a ceremony was held at Madison Square Garden to commemorate Robinson's retirement, all the middleweight champions that he had fought were invited, save for LaMotta, who was present, but not allowed to be introduced to the crowd. LaMotta would later get the chance to tell his own side of the story in his autobiography *Raging Bull*. It provided the basis for the Oscar-winning movie of the same name, in which the boxer was played by Robert De Niro.

The popular Italian-American middleweight Rocky Graziano poses in the ring. He fought Ray Robinson for the world title in 1952 but lost in three rounds.

A hard right from Sugar Ray Robinson puts light heavyweight champion Joey Maxim on the back foot during their gruelling title fight in 1952. Exhausted by the effort of fighting in the extreme heat, Robinson quit before the 14th round.

After winning a series of non-title bouts in early 1947, Robinson defended his title for the first time on 24 June. His opponent was Jimmy Doyle. Before the fight, Robinson dreamt that he would kill Doyle in the ring and had to be talked out of withdrawing from the contest. The prophecy came true. When the Californian fighter was knocked down in the eighth, he tried to get up, but collapsed back on to the canvas. He died in hospital the next day. The tragedy had a profound psychological effect on Robinson, who set up a trust fund to support his opponent's mother.

Sugar Ray Robinson's reign as welterweight champion was to last for more than four years.

However, even though Robinson fought 47 times during this period, he only actually defended the welterweight belt five times. The most notable of these fights came against the crowd-pleasing Cuban boxer Kid Gavilan. In an earlier non-title fight, a controversial decision had gone to Robinson, and many observers expected Gavilan to prevail in the rematch. However, after trailing in the early stages of the fight, Robinson managed to rally in the later rounds to earn a clear decision win.

The majority of the contests that Robinson fought during his time as welterweight champion were non-title fights held at the 73kg (160lb) middleweight limit. It was not surprising, then, that in 1951 he should give up his belt to fight for the middleweight crown. His opponent in the contest would be a familiar one: Jake LaMotta.

Shortly after the bout with LaMotta, Robinson headed for Europe for a series of fights. Robinson took with him both a sizeable entourage and his trademark pink Cadillac. After contests in France, Switzerland, Belgium, Germany and Italy, Robinson travelled to London to face Randolph Turpin in what was to be the only title defence of the tour. Robinson prepared for the fight largely by playing golf and his lackadaisical approach cost him

Sugar Ray Robinson tap dances at the French Casino nightclub in New York in November, 1952. After his first retirement, Robinson attempted to begin a career as an entertainer.

During a ceremony held to celebrate his career, Sugar Ray Robinson (centre) is held aloft by four of his most famous opponents, (from left) Randy Turpin, Gene Fullmer, Carmen Basilio and Bobo Olson.

when the tough and unorthodox Turpin was given the decision. It was only Robinson's second loss in 133 contests.

The rematch with Turpin was held on 12 September 1951 at the Polo Grounds, New York City. Turpin again proved to be a tough opponent for Robinson and the first nine rounds of the fight were fairly even. In the 10th round, however, a clash of heads caused a cut to open up above Robinson's left eye, forcing him to go on a ferocious offensive that forced the referee to stop the contest. The middleweight crown was back in American hands.

After the Turpin rematch, Robinson did not fight again for six months, returning to the ring in March 1952 for a lacklustre win over Bobo Olson. He then turned his attentions to former middleweight champion Rocky Graziano, a hard-hitting, rugged Italian-American. For the brief duration of the fight he caused Robinson plenty of problems, knocking him down with a hard shot in the third round. Unfortunately for Graziano, Robinson got straight back up to knock him out.

Robinson now moved up in weight again to fight light heavyweight champion Joey Maxim. The contest was held at Yankee Stadium, New York, on 25 June 1952 in unbearably humid conditions – the temperature exceeded 38°C (100°F). The first victim of the conditions was the referee, who had to be replaced midway through the fight. The second was Robinson, who was forced to quit from heat exhaustion after the 13th round, despite having had the better of the contest until then. Later that year, Robinson announced his retirement from boxing.

After quitting the fight game, Sugar Ray embarked on a second career as a dancer, hoping that his fame and popularity would guarantee the venture's success. However, the novelty appeal of his stage appearances soon wore off. To make matters worse, problems began to crop up with the various businesses that Robinson owned in Harlem. As his financial difficulties mounted, Sugar Ray returned to the one place where he knew he could make money: the ring.

The early stage of Robinson's post-retirement career consisted largely of a series of fights in which he won, lost and then regained the middleweight championship. He returned to boxing in 1955, and after a largely successful series of warm-up fights, took on Bobo Olson for the title. Robinson knocked Olson out in the second round, and made similarly short work of him in the rematch. Robinson next defended his title against Gene Fullmer in January 1957 at Madison Square Garden, losing by decision. He regained the title by a fifth-round knockout four months later. Two epic fights against the squat, muscular Carmen Basilio followed.

Sugar Ray Robinson is knocked outside the ring by Gene Fullmer in the seventh round of their fight in January, 1957. Robinson lost by decision. The pair fought four times in total.

Both were decided by split decision. Basilio edged the first, while Robinson prevailed in the rematch, winning the middleweight title for an unprecedented fifth time in the process.

The bout with Basilio would prove to be Robinson's last successful title fight. He lost the middleweight crown to the unfancied Paul Pender in 1960 and three more title shots – one against Pender and two against Fullmer – proved fruitless. He continued fighting until 1965, sometimes for purses of less than $1,000, but the defeats became more frequent. Eventually, after a decision loss against Joey Archer in November 1965, he retired for a second and final time.

Ironically, for someone who had been one of the richest and most successful athletes of his age, Robinson spent most of his retirement battling ill health and attempting to stave off financial problems. He died on 12 April 1989. Many offered tributes to him, but the most succinct probably came from his frequent opponent Bobo Olson. "He was the greatest boxer to ever step into the ring", he said. "He was the best. I tried to copy his style a few times, but I couldn't do it. He was too good."

Sugar Ray Robinson lands a hard right to the jaw of Carmen Basilio in their world title fight in September, 1957. Robinson lost on a split decision, but won the rematch six months later.

Rocky Marciano

The career of Rocky Marciano is summed up by a single statistic. Unlike all the other great heavyweight champions of the twentieth century, Marciano never lost as a professional, finishing with an unblemished record of 49 wins and no defeats. This feat alone has cemented his place as one of the sport's immortals. Rocco Francis Marchegiano was born on 1 September 1923 in Brockton, Massachusetts. He grew up in a poor Italian-American neighbourhood. His father worked in a shoe factory and the family's struggle against poverty would provide a powerful incentive during Marciano's boxing career.

Marciano never boxed as a boy, preferring to play baseball, and his first taste of the ring came after he joined the army in 1943. His amateur record was far from unblemished. In his first fight, a badly out-of-shape Marciano was comprehensively outboxed and then disqualified after kneeing his opponent in the stomach. A patchy and somewhat disjointed amateur career followed. He reached the finals of a tournament in Portland, Oregon, but lost the final after injuring his hand. He fought for the first time as a professional in early 1947, but after winning this contest in three rounds, he turned back to his boyhood love: baseball. However, a tryout for the Chicago Cubs ended in failure, forcing Marciano to resume his boxing career, albeit in the amateur rather than the professional ranks. After more mixed results, Marciano turned his back on the unpaid game for good in the summer of 1948.

Marciano's amateur record – an undistinguished eight wins and four losses – offered no hint of the greatness that was to follow. Nor did his style or physique. At just over 1.78m (5ft 10in) and around 86kg (190lb), Marciano was small for a heavyweight, even by the standards of the 1940s. Technically, he was extremely crude. However, what Marciano did possess was natural knockout power – "heavy hands" in boxing parlance.

Rocky Marciano was one of the great icons of 1950s America. His aggressive style endeared him to a generation of boxing fans.

When allied to a constant willingness to attack and an ability to absorb punishment, this power was enough to propel him to the heights of the boxing world.

Marciano won his second professional bout in July 1948 by first-round stoppage and continued in the same vein for the remainder of the year. Ten more opponents had been dispatched by Christmas, and of these only one had made it past the second round. Marciano was helped in his rise by veteran trainer Charley Goldman, a former bantamweight who had enjoyed a successful career in the early years of the twentieth century.

Goldman was allied to manager Al Weill, whose extensive web of connections was equally important to Marciano's career. Weill was responsible for removing a syllable from Rocky's name, figuring that "Marchegiano" was too difficult for the general public to pronounce.

Marciano's career continued on its upwards trajectory in 1949. Fighting largely in Rhode Island, the so-called "Brockton Blockbuster" put together a string of 13 straight victories, knocking out many of his opponents in the first round. Although the manner of Marciano's

Rocky Marciano (right) works out with trainer Charley Goldman in October, 1951, shortly before his fight with former world champion Joe Louis. Goldman was instrumental in shaping Marciano's fighting style.

wins was impressive, the quality of his opposition was often questionable. This situation changed in March 1950, when he took on fellow Italian-American Roland LaStarza at Madison Square Garden.

Unlike most of the boxers that Marciano had faced, LaStarza was a genuine prospect. At the time of the fight, LaStarza's record stood at 37 wins and no losses. A highly skilled defensive boxer, he was in many ways the mirror image of Marciano. The contest proved to be the closest of Marciano's career. Although he managed to knock LaStarza down in the fourth round, his opponent recovered and succeeded in outboxing

him for much of the remainder of the contest. At the end of the allotted 10 rounds, one judge awarded the contest to Marciano, while the other gave it to LaStarza. Referee Jack Watson cast his deciding vote in favour of Rocky. The decision did not sit well with LaStarza, who was convinced that he had done enough to earn the win. He would get another chance to defeat Marciano, but not for some time.

Marciano continued to impress over the course of the next two years. While some of Marciano's opponents during this period were clearly overmatched, many provided him with stern tests. Ted Lowry, who had taken

Rocky Marciano turns his back on former champion Joe Louis after knocking him down in the eighth round of their 1951 fight. The contest was the last of Louis's distinguished career.

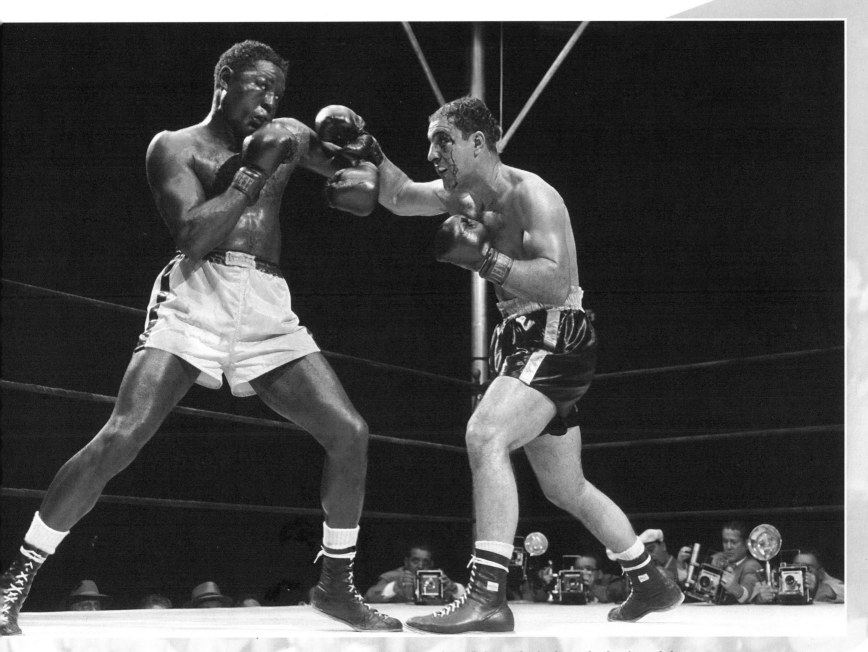

With blood pouring from his eye, Rocky Marciano (right) attacks Ezzard Charles in the 14th round of their June 1954 encounter. Charles proved to be one of Marciano's toughest opponents.

Marciano the distance in 1949, repeated the feat in 1950. Another stiff challenge was presented by Rex Layne. Layne's record of 37 fights with only one loss meant that he went into his July 1951 contest with Marciano as favourite. Layne fought well in the earlier rounds, but Marciano's power soon began to tell. The fight ended with a knockout in the sixth of the 10 scheduled rounds.

In October 1951 Marciano took part in his most high-profile contest to date when he took on former champion Joe Louis. Forced out of retirement by a desperate need for finances, Louis was by now only a fraction of the fighter who had utterly dominated the heavyweight scene for over a decade. It was a fight that Marciano did not want – like many men of his generation he had once idolized Louis – but had to take. Although the older boxer fought bravely, he was no match for Marciano. In the eighth round Marciano dropped Louis once before clubbing him through the ropes with a barrage of hooks. The fight brought an end to Louis's career.

Marciano took little pleasure in the win – he is alleged to have cried in the dressing room after the fight – but it

59

MARCIANO

WALCOTT

In September 1952 the world heavyweight title was held by the veteran Jersey Joe Walcott. Walcott had begun boxing 22 years earlier and had only finally claimed the crown in July 1951 with a knockout win over Ezzard Charles. Incredibly, it was Walcott's fifth shot at the title. He had failed twice against Joe Louis and twice against Charles. After winning the championship, he defended it once – Charles was again the opponent – before turning to the obvious challenger: Rocky Marciano.

The fight between Walcott and Marciano took place at the Municipal Stadium, Philadelphia, on 23 September 1952. There was a huge difference in age between the two men. According to the official records Marciano was nine years younger than his opponent, though many believed that Walcott was even older than his alleged 38 years and seven months. Nevertheless, the champion was confident that his greater skill would be enough to see off a challenger he saw as a crude brawler.

A right hand from Rocky Marciano glances off the head of Jersey Joe Walcott during the pair's world title fight in September 1952.

To begin with, Walcott's confidence seemed justified. He dropped Marciano in the first round with a short left hook – the first time that the Brockton fighter had been down in his entire career. However, the challenger got up quickly and for the next few rounds held his own in a bruising encounter fought mainly at close range. Marciano suffered a second setback in the sixth round when a clash of heads saw both fighters cut. Some solution used to stem the flow of blood ended up in Marciano's eye, causing him to have difficulties seeing. Again, however, Rocky recovered.

As the fight wore on, Walcott slowly began to impose himself. He was particularly dominant in the 11th round, when a series of combinations badly cut the challenger. By the beginning of the 13th, Marciano was bruised, battered and behind on points. However, he managed to save the contest with a single punch. Backing Walcott into the ropes he unleashed a short right hand – a punch he called his "Suzie Q" – that caught his opponent flush on the jaw. Walcott sank momentarily to his knee and then collapsed face first on to the canvas, his left hand draped over the bottom rope. Marciano was the new champion.

Rocky Marciano struggles to return to his feet after being knocked down in the first round of his first fight against Jersey Joe Walcott. Marciano came back to win the contest in the 13th round.

considerably increased his profile. Four straight victories the following year brought him a shot at the ultimate prize in the sport, the world heavyweight title.

Marciano's defeat of Jersey Joe Walcott in September 1952 was named Fight of the Year by the magazine *The Ring*. The rematch, held just under eight months later in Chicago, was an anticlimax. It resembled its predecessor only in the manner of its conclusion. Again, the fight was ended by a short right from Marciano that left Walcott unconscious. This time, however, the punch came just two minutes and 25 seconds into the first round.

In September, Marciano turned his attentions to an old adversary, Roland LaStarza. LaStarza was still resentful of the outcome of the first meeting between the pair and his continued insistence that he had been robbed added an edge to the contest. Like the earlier bout, the 1953 fight was characterized by a contrast in style, pitting a boxer against a brawler. For the first six rounds, LaStarza used his greater skill and mobility to keep Marciano at distance. The champion kept on coming forward, however, and gradually the constant bombardment of hooks began to take its toll. By the ninth round, Marciano was hitting the challenger at will. In the 11th, he knocked LaStarza clean through the ropes. The challenger recovered, only for the referee to stop the contest seconds later.

After the LaStarza fight, Marciano took a break of almost nine months before returning to the ring to take on former champion Ezzard Charles in what was to

Ezzard Charles (right) reacts to a hard left hook from Rocky Marciano in the first round of their June 1954 fight in New York. Marciano eventually won in the 15th round.

Rocky Marciano (left) lands a punch to the midsection of Englishman Don Cockell. Cockell managed to survive until the ninth round of their fight in 1955.

Rocky Marciano (left) and Archie Moore trade punches in their 1955 heavyweight title fight, the last contest of Marciano's career. Light heavyweight champion Moore was unable to collect a title in a second weight class.

prove one of the most physically demanding fights of his career. Known as the "Cincinnati Cobra", Charles had spent much of his early career fighting at middleweight and light heavyweight, but various circumstances had denied him a title shot at either of these weights. He had eventually emerged as heavyweight champion in the vacuum left by the first retirement of Joe Louis.

When Marciano met Charles in New York on 17 June 1954, Charles was the older man by just over two years. However, Charles had endured a more physically demanding career. It was the challenger's 94th professional contest, as opposed to Marciano's 46th, and his resumé was not peppered with untaxing first-round knockout victories. For this reason, many believed that

Charles was past his best. While this may have been partially true, the Cincinnati fighter still proved good enough to dominate much of the early part of the 15-round contest. Marciano rallied later and did just enough to shade a close decision.

A rematch was inevitable. The pair met for a second time just three months later, again in New York. Marciano began well, dropping Charles in the second and keeping up the pressure in the following three rounds. However, in the sixth a punch from Charles split Marciano's nose open. Attempts to staunch the flow of blood failed, and at the beginning of the eighth round, Rocky was sent out with a simple set of instructions from his corner: knock him out now or the fight will be stopped. Halfway through the round a clubbing right hand from Marciano knocked Charles to the canvas. The challenger got back up, but Marciano sensed his chance and unleashed a barrage of punches to bring the contest to a conclusion.

After a defence against the game but limited Englishman Don Cockell, Marciano stepped up for what would be the final fight of his career on 21 September 1955. His opponent was Archie Moore, a veteran fighter with 176 contests to his name. The reigning light heavyweight champion of the world, Moore was able to knock Marciano to the canvas in the second round, but like Jersey Joe Walcott three years previously, paid a high price for his temporary triumph. He was knocked down five times in total, the final blows coming in the ninth round.

Marciano retired seven months later, weary of the increasing amounts of time he was spending away from his family. Also, he had witnessed at first hand the sad spectacle of the once-great Joe Louis being fed to younger fighters on the rise. It was a fate that he was determined to avoid himself.

After quitting the ring Marciano presented a boxing show on television and made money from personal appearances. However, he was not destined to enjoy a long retirement. On 31 August 1969, on the eve of his 46th birthday, he boarded a private plane bound for Des Moines, Iowa, where he was due to be a guest at a fight. Adverse weather conditions forced the inexperienced pilot to attempt an emergency landing, a manoeuvre he fatally misjudged, guiding the plane into a tree. Both the pilot and Marciano were killed on impact.

The remains of the light aircraft that carried Rocky Marciano to his death. The plane crashed in a field in Iowa after the pilot lost control.

Muhammad Ali

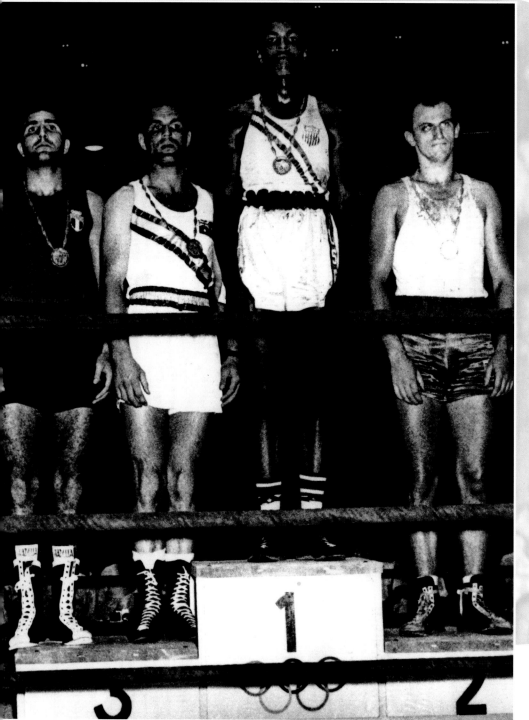

Known simply as the "Greatest", Muhammad Ali was one of the most iconic figures of the twentieth century. His controversial stand against the Vietnam War and advocacy of black nationalism thrust him into the political spotlight at one of the most turbulent times in the history of the United States. However, Ali's ring achievements alone would be enough to secure him a place among the greatest sportsmen of all time. An Olympic gold medallist, he went on to become the first boxer to win the heavyweight title three times.

Muhammad Ali was born Cassius Marcellus Clay on 17 January 1942 in Louisville, Kentucky. The name would eventually be jettisoned in 1964 after Ali's conversion to Islam, but it was the one under which he fought for the formative years of his career. The story of Ali's introduction to boxing has entered the sport's folklore. The theft of his bicycle forced a 12-year-old Ali to search out the nearest policeman. It so happened that the nearest policeman, Joe Martin, was teaching boys to box in a local gym. When Ali told Martin what he was going to do to the person who stole his bike, Martin suggested that it would be a good idea if he learned how to fight first.

The young Ali progressed quickly under Martin's tutelage and a host of amateur titles followed. The success led to Ali being selected to represent the United States at the 1960 Rome Olympics. Even at this stage of his career, Ali was being hailed as a potential star, with magazine articles celebrating both his natural charisma and his idiosyncratic style of fighting. Ali liked to keep his hands low, floating out of the way of blows rather than absorbing them on his gloves. This graceful, dancing style would be a trademark of the first half of his career and was enough to secure him a gold medal.

Ali turned professional on returning home, opening his professional career in October 1960 with a six-round decision win over Tunney Hunsaker, a policeman from

Muhammad Ali (centre, then known as Cassius Clay) stands on the winner's podium at the 1960 Olympic Games. He is flanked by the silver and bronze medallists.

champion was cut in the third round, but in the fourth, the fight took an unexpected turn. Ali suddenly experienced problems with his vision. He returned to his corner complaining that some chemical (possibly that used to treat Liston's cuts) was burning his eyes, and asked to be pulled from the fight.

The history of boxing would have been very different if Dundee had obeyed his fighter. Instead he rinsed Ali's eyes out with water and pushed him back into the ring, ordering him to try to survive the round. Fortunately for Ali, his vision soon cleared. The sixth round belonged to Ali and, at its conclusion, the fight took another unexpected twist. Liston quit, complaining of an injured shoulder. Ali immediately began to dance around the ring, searching out his doubters in the crowd and volubly reminding them of his status as the "Greatest".

The first contest against Sonny Liston would be the last that Ali would fight as Cassius Clay. Less than two

Muhammad Ali (right) makes his professional debut against Tunney Hunsaker in Louisville, Kentucky, in October, 1960. Ali won in six rounds.

Sonny Liston (right) ducks under a punch from Muhammad Ali during the fifth round of their first title fight. Liston quit on his stool after the sixth round.

West Virginia. Teaming up with trainer Angelo Dundee, who would stay with him for the rest of his career, Ali won his next 18 contests. During this period he built up a reputation for showmanship. His habit of predicting the results of his upcoming fights and general playful boastfulness endeared him to some sections of the public, but riled others. Nevertheless, by the autumn of 1963 he had established himself as a genuine contender for the world heavyweight crown, then held by the formidable Sonny Liston.

The task facing any fighter hoping to dethrone Liston seemed immense. The champion's two first-round demolitions of Floyd Patterson had made him appear unbeatable. However, Ali refused to be intimidated by the opponent whom he derided as the "big ugly bear". A calculated campaign of taunts led to Liston accepting Ali's challenge.

The two fighters met on 25 February 1964 in Miami, Florida. It immediately became clear that the fight would be less one-sided than most boxing insiders had predicted. Ali used his superior speed to duck in and out of range, avoiding most of Liston's attacks, while simultaneously causing damage of his own. The

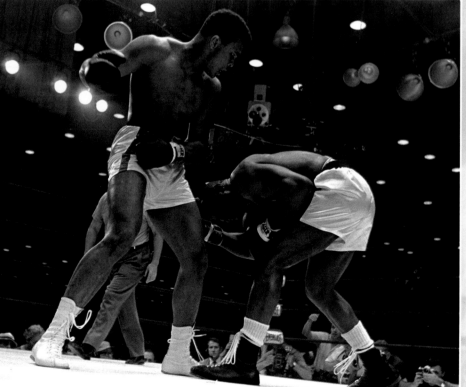

Muhammad Ali (left) taunts Sonny Liston after knocking him down in the first round of their rematch. Ali is restrained by referee Jersey Joe Walcott.

Muhammad Ali (left) reacts to a punch thrown by former heavyweight champion Floyd Patterson. Ali won a match that was marked by bad blood between the two men.

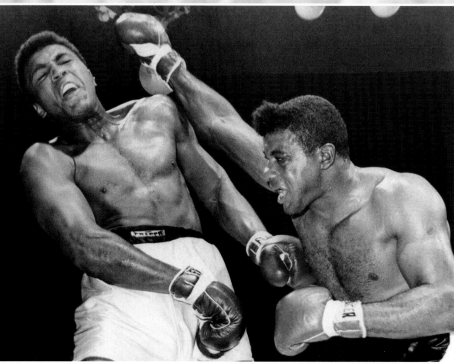

weeks later, he assumed the name Muhammad Ali, which had been bestowed upon him by Elijah Muhammad, the leader of the Nation of Islam (NOI). The NOI was a radical black nationalist organization that espoused racial separatism. Ali had first come into contact with its members in 1961 and had become increasingly drawn to its teachings. However, he only publicly acknowledged his affiliation to the group in a press conference held in the wake of the Liston fight. Ali's show of allegiance to the NOI led to his popularity plummeting among many sections of US society.

The unsatisfactory ending to the championship fight with Liston made a rematch inevitable. The fight, held in May 1965, proved to be both short and controversial. Around halfway through the first round, Ali threw a punch that knocked Liston to the canvas. The speed of the shot meant that many in the crowd missed it, prompting rumours that Liston had taken a dive, either on the orders of the mafia, which had close connections with his management, or because he feared reprisals from the Nation of Islam. The theories were dismissed by many closely involved in the contest, but persisted decades later.

Ali followed up his victory over Liston with a fight with another former champion, Floyd Patterson, who was stopped after 12 rounds. Ali's next four defences were contested overseas, but he returned to the United States before the end of 1966 to deliver one of the key performances of his career. While some of his later fights were more celebrated, it was his contest against Cleveland Williams that saw him at the height of his powers. In the two and a half rounds that the fight lasted, Ali demonstrated all of his skill, grace and power, gliding around the ring while hitting his opponent at will. Williams was knocked down four times before the referee intervened.

Ali fought twice in 1967. In February he delivered a brutal beating to Ernie Terrell, who had infuriated the champion during the build-up by repeatedly referring to him as "Clay" rather than "Ali". The following month saw a routine win over the veteran Zora Folley. The most notable aspect of the fight was that it was the last that Ali would take part in for three and a half years.

In 1966, a change in the law regarding eligibility for the US armed forces had raised the possibility of Ali being sent to fight in the Vietnam War. Ali had responded by claiming to be a conscientious objector,

Muhammad Ali (left) celebrates after knocking out Cleveland Williams. Ali completely dominated the fight, delivering one of his greatest performances.

Muhammad Ali looks down at opponent Zora Folley in March, 1967. The fight would be the last that Ali would contest for three and a half years.

Muhammad Ali (right) shouts "What's my name?" at challenger Ernie Terrell during their February 1967 bout. Terrell had refused to call Ali by his Muslim name, and called him "Clay" instead.

famously declaring "I ain't got no quarrel with them Vietcong." His stance became official on 28 April 1967, when he refused to step forward at an induction ceremony held in Houston, Texas. Ali was subsequently stripped of his boxing licence by every state athletic commission in the country. Ali spent his years in exile from the boxing ring touring the country, giving lectures on university campuses. During this period he became the public face of the growing anti-war movement, a hate figure in many quarters but a hero in others.

Ali returned to the ring in October 1970, when he beat Jerry Quarey in Atlanta, Georgia. The fight was only able to take place because there was no boxing commission in the state. However, later that year a successful challenge to Ali's national ban cleared the way for a full-scale return.

Joe Frazier (right) delivers a punch to the face of Muhammad Ali during the first of their three encounters. Frazier won the 1971 fight to hand Ali his first ever professional defeat.

A win over Oscar Bonavena set Ali up for a match against the man who had been crowned heavyweight champion in his absence: Joe Frazier. The contest would be the first instalment of one of the great rivalries in the history of sport. Billed as "The Fight of the Century", it pitched two unbeaten champions against one another, each of whom would be paid the then unheard of sum of $2.5 million for his participation.

The fight took place at New York's Madison Square Garden on 8 March 1971. Ali no longer possessed the speed he displayed in his 1960s heyday, but still moved well enough to shade the early rounds. However, as the fight wore on, the strength of the squat, bull-like Frazier began to tell. A knockdown by Frazier in the final round sealed Ali's fate. Frazier was given the decision. Ali's unbeaten run was at an end.

Ali now embarked on a long campaign to regain his crown. A series of 10 wins followed over the course of the next two years before Ali ran into the tough, unorthodox Ken Norton. Just two rounds into the contest,

ALI

FOREMAN

Muhammad Ali's 1974 fight with George Foreman had strong echoes of his clash with Sonny Liston some 10 years earlier. Once again, Ali was confronted by a champion who was seen as unbeatable in many quarters. Like Liston, Foreman did not outbox his rivals, he simply destroyed them by brute force. A comparison of the fates of recent opponents did not bode well for Ali. Ali had boxed 51 rounds with Ken Norton and Joe Frazier, winning two close decisions and losing the other two. By contrast, Foreman had brushed both men aside with ease. Each had lasted two rounds. Between them, Norton and Frazier had been knocked down nine times in less than 11 minutes.

The reputations of the two combatants would have made the fight between Ali and Foreman a huge event wherever it was held. However, the fact that it took place in Zaire gave the contest a historic significance. No sporting event of this size had ever been held in Africa, and the setting had particular relevance for the black nationalist Ali. The venue for the fight had been the brainchild of the promoter Don King, who, having offered the two fighters $10 million between them, had needed someone to bankroll the event. He found a willing ally in President Mobutu Sese Seko, who saw the fight as a way of putting his country on the world stage.

After a delay caused by a cut suffered by Foreman in training, the "Rumble in the Jungle" eventually began at 4.00 am on the morning of 30 October. Going into the fight, the conventional wisdom had been that Ali would try to dance away from his more powerful opponent. For the first three minutes, the fight followed this pattern, but from the second round onward, Ali began to employ unexpected and seemingly suicidal tactics. Rather than use his agility to stay out of reach, he retreated to the ropes, where he absorbed wave upon wave of punishment. As the rounds wore on, Foreman began to tire, allowing Ali to counterattack. Then, suddenly, in the eighth round, Ali launched a barrage of punches that left Foreman defenceless on the canvas. At age 32, Ali had recaptured the heavyweight crown.

Muhammad Ali (right) launches an attack on George Foreman during their 1974 contest in Zaire. The unbeaten Foreman was an overwhelming favourite for the match.

George Foreman struggles to rise to his feet after being knocked down by Muhammad Ali. Ali's eighth-round recovery is seen as one of the great comebacks in the history of sport.

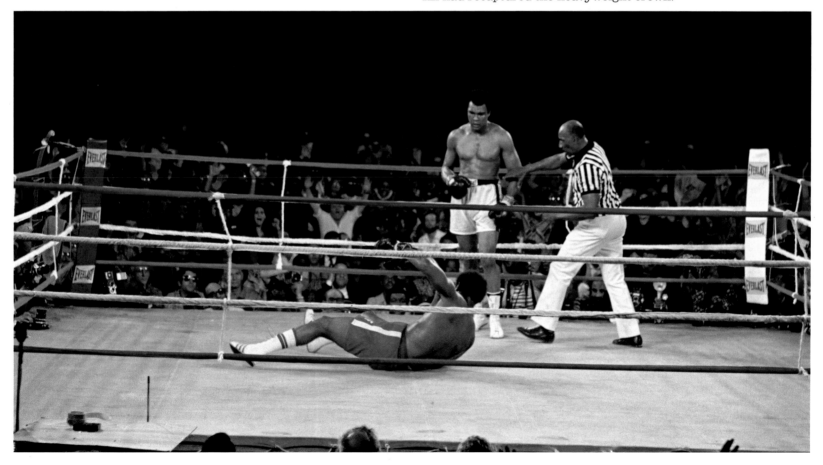

a straight right from Norton broke Ali's jaw. Ali fought on bravely, but lost on a split decision. Nevertheless, an equally narrow win in the return match set up a second encounter with Frazier.

The animosity that had existed between the two fighters at the time of the first contest had grown considerably in the intervening period and a pre-fight television appearance descended into a brawl. The fight itself was the least compelling of their three contests, but Ali's decision win earned him the right to fight the man who had taken away Frazier's championship belt: George Foreman.

After defeating Foreman, Ali defended the title three times before meeting his old rival Joe Frazier in the Philippines on 1 October 1975. Promoted as the "Thrilla in Manila", the clash would prove to be the most celebrated of the pair's three contests. One of the most notable aspects of the event was its bitter build-up. Ali made a habit of insulting his opponents before a

Muhammad Ali (left) and Joe Frazier flank boxing promoter Don King shortly after the announcement that the pair would fight for a third time. Ali taunts Frazier; the champion's constant verbal attacks on his opponent would be a key feature of the build-up to the fight.

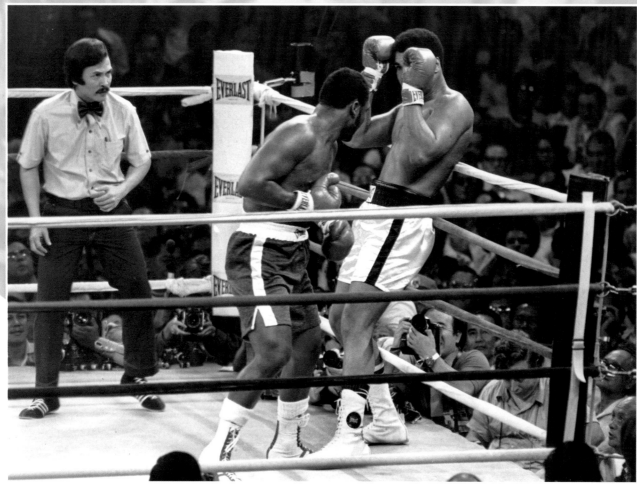

Joe Frazier (left) launches an assault at a defensive Muhammad Ali during the "Thrilla in Manila". By the end of the 14th round, a battered Frazier could no longer see. He was withdrawn by his corner.

Muhammad Ali throws a right to the jaw of Ken Norton during their 1973 rematch. Norton had won their first meeting. It was only the second loss of Ali's career.

fight, but usually his taunts were good-humoured. In Manila, however, a line was crossed. Frazier was derided as ugly and stupid, and constantly compared to an ape. The result was that by the time he set foot in the ring, Frazier was motivated by pure hatred.

The fight was held at 10.45am. The scheduling helped to maximize viewing figures in the United States, but ensured that the bout was held in incredibly humid conditions. The fight was contested with relentless brutality, ebbing and flowing as first Ali and then Frazier dominated. Ali regained control in the 11th and peppered Frazier's face with shots for the next three rounds. By the end of the 14th, Frazier could hardly see, and his trainer, Eddie Futch, called the fight off to protect him. Unbeknown to either of them, Ali may not have been able to carry on either. He collapsed before the result could be announced.

The third fight with Joe Frazier would have proved a fitting climax to Ali's career, but instead he fought on, his powers slowly waning. After three fights against

Larry Holmes (left) lands a heavy blow to the body of Muhammad Ali. Slow and cumbersome, Ali offered minimal resistance in the penultimate contest of his career.

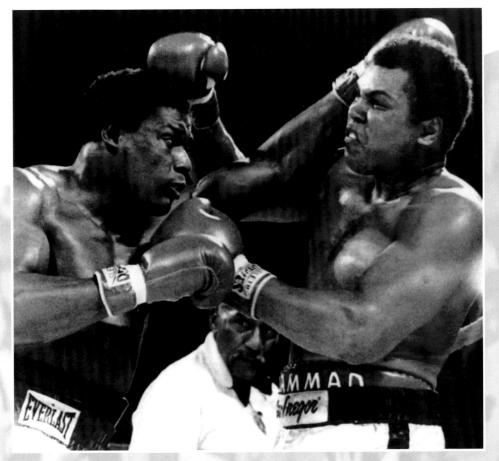

2 October 1980 to fight Larry Holmes. Holmes hit a slow and lethargic Ali at will, forcing Angelo Dundee to throw in the towel at the end of the 10th round. Ali, convinced that his bad performance had been the result of some incorrectly prescribed drugs, fought once more a year later, against Trevor Berbick. The "Drama in Bahama" failed to live up to its name. A one-sided loss provided an unfitting end to a great career.

In retirement, Ali's health worsened still further. He was soon diagnosed with Parkinson's Syndrome, a condition caused by the punishment he had suffered in the ring. He retreated to his farm in Michigan, where he spent his days studying the Koran. Nevertheless, a number of high-profile appearances, most notably a central role in the opening ceremony of the 1996 Atlanta Olympics, kept him in the public eye. His status as both a great fighter and a key figure in American history remained undiminished in the early part of the twenty-first century.

Muhammad Ali's final fight came against Trevor Berbick (left) in the Bahamas in 1981. Berbick won a comfortable decision.

Muhammad Ali is pictured in 2006. By this time, Ali had been suffering from Parkinson's Syndrome for more than 20 years.

journeymen opponents, Ali won an extremely lucky decision victory against Ken Norton. Further wins over Alfredo Evangelista and the hard-hitting Earnie Shavers followed, but then disaster struck. In February 1978 Ali was paired with Leon Spinks, a young, barely rated fighter with just seven fights under his belt. A slow and out-of-shape Ali was unable to keep up with his younger opponent and lost a 15-round decision.

A rematch with Spinks was hastily arranged for September. Weeks of hard training did little to improve Ali, but fortunately for him, the wildly undisciplined Spinks had spent the intervening seven months partying. He came into the ring in even worse shape than Ali. A unanimous decision victory meant that Ali had become the first man to win the heavyweight championship of the world three times, yet the manner of his victory diluted the magnitude of the achievement.

Ali promptly retired. There were soon signs of a deterioration in his health, most noticeably a slowing of his speech and a problem with coordination. Despite these difficulties, Ali came back out of retirement on

Roberto Duran

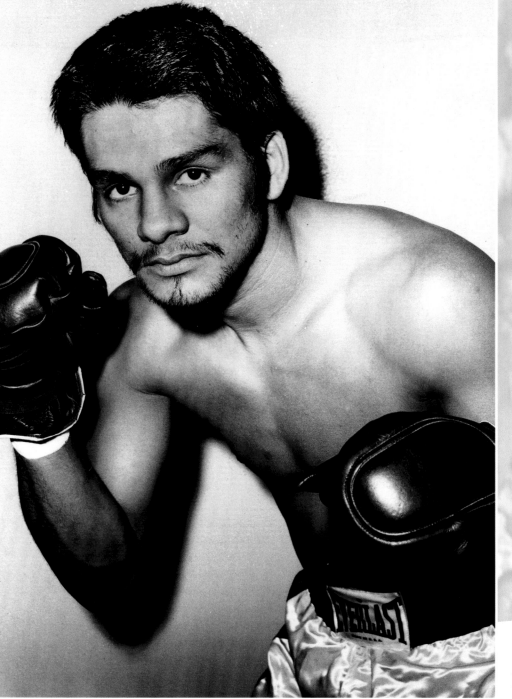

The 33-year ring career of the Panamanian boxer Roberto Duran embraced extreme highs and bitter lows, and elicited both adulation and ridicule from his countrymen. Revelling in the nickname "Hands of Stone", he was one of the sport's greatest ever lightweight champions. Roberto Duran Samaniego was born in El Corrillo, Panama, on 16 June 1951. Because his mother was unable to support the family financially, he spent part of his childhood begging for change on the streets. Duran first stepped into a boxing gym at age eight and was fighting competitively a year later. His amateur career was successful but brief. Poverty forced Duran to make an early entry into the paid ranks, and he was only 16 years old when he made his professional debut, beating Carlos Mendoza by unanimous decision in February 1968.

For the first three years of his career, Duran campaigned almost entirely in Panama. His first experience of fighting in the United States came in September 1971, by which time he had built up a record of 24 straight wins. That night, Duran knocked out Benny Huertas at Madison Square Garden in just one minute and six seconds of the first round. The following June, Duran would return to the venue, where he would compete for the lightweight championship of the world.

After defeating Ken Buchanan to win the world lightweight title, Duran went back to Panama a national hero. Two victories in non-title fights quickly followed, before Duran returned to Madison Square Garden to take on the Puerto Rican Esteban De Jesus. Again, Duran's lightweight title was not at stake, which proved fortunate for the Panamanian. De Jesus knocked Duran down in the first round before going on to win a unanimous decision. Rumours abounded that Duran's preparations for the fight were not as diligent as they should have been. Similar stories would surface throughout his career.

A young Roberto Duran poses for the cameras. The Panamanian won numerous titles in a professional career that spanned more than 20 years.

DURAN

BUCHANAN

When Roberto Duran beat Benny Huertas in New York in 1971, he was not the only Panamanian fighting that night. Duran's bout was merely one of several on the undercard of the contest between his fellow countryman Ismael Laguna and the Scot Ken Buchanan. Buchanan had taken the World Boxing Association (WBA) lightweight title from Laguna in Puerto Rico the previous year, but only by way of a split decision. The rematch also went the distance, but once again Buchanan prevailed.

Duran would soon get an opportunity to avenge his hero and compatriot. By the spring of 1972 Duran had built up a record of 28 consecutive wins. This sequence had established him as the number one contender for Buchanan's title and the pair duly met at Madison Square Garden on 26 June 1972. Because all but four of Duran's contests had taken place in Panama, many amongst the crowd were unfamiliar with the 21-year-old prodigy. Duran did not take long to make an impression on them. Within seconds of the opening bell, Buchanan had been knocked to the canvas.

The Scot recovered quickly, and attempted to capitalize on his superior height and reach by keeping the challenger at bay with his jab. His efforts had little effect. An aggressive Duran repeatedly closed the distance to ensure that the contest was fought predominately at close quarters. The sheer ferocity of Duran's assaults gradually took their toll and by the 12th round Buchanan was well behind on points.

Duran was virtually guaranteed victory, but would eventually achieve it in controversial circumstances. As the bell rang for the end of the 13th round, Duran threw one last punch, which landed in Buchanan's groin. The Scotsman collapsed immediately and, still in agony at the beginning of the next round, was unable to continue. The referee, Johnny LoBianco, had been separating the fighters when the punch occurred and had not seen it, and so

awarded the match, and the championship belt, to Duran.

For Buchanan, the punch had long-lasting consequences. The blow severely damaged one of his testicles and the injury still caused him pain decades later.

Ken Buchanan (left) winces in pain as Roberto Duran lands a punch to his groin at the end of the 13th round of their world title fight. Buchanan was unable to continue when the bell rang for the following round.

Equally long-lasting was his belief that his title had been stolen from him, a feeling compounded by the fact that he never received the opportunity to avenge himself in a rematch.

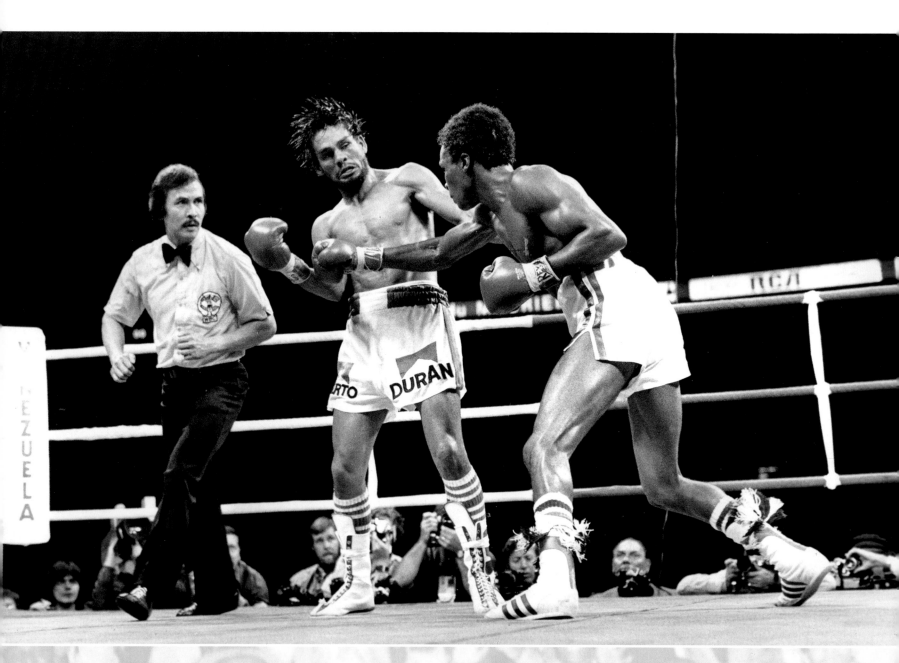

The setback proved to be very temporary. Just two months later, in January 1973, Duran made his first successful defence of his title when he knocked out Jimmy Robertson in five rounds in Panama City. Duran's reign as lightweight champion continued for another six years. During this time, he defended his crown a further 11 times and also fought numerous non-title contests. Among his most notable bouts were two stoppage victories against his only conqueror, Esteban De Jesus.

Duran's second win over De Jesus proved to be his last title contest at lightweight. By the late 1970s, Duran was having a problem making the division's 61kg (135lb) limit, and many of his non-title fights were occurring at welterweight (67kg or 147lb). Realizing that he could no longer make the lower weight, Duran gave up his lightweight belt in January 1979. After five consecutive victories at the higher weight, he then took on the current welterweight champion Sugar Ray Leonard.

Duran would fight Leonard twice in 1980 and the two contests would mark the high and low points of his career respectively. The first took place in Montreal,

Roberto Duran (left) reacts to a right hand from Sugar Ray Leonard during the Brawl in Montreal. Duran won the fight to claim the WBC world welterweight title.

Canada, on 20 June. Duran spent much of the prefight build-up goading the American, and the attacks unsettled Leonard. Leonard was the more skilful boxer and in order to win he needed to fight cleanly at range. However, affected by Duran's taunts, he elected to try to outbrawl him. Leonard's tactics ensured that the fight was perfectly tailored to Duran's strengths and the Panamanian muscled his way to a unanimous decision victory.

The two fighters reacted to the outcome of the match in contrasting fashions. While Duran headed to the discos of Panama City to celebrate, Leonard went straight back to the gym, where he prepared for the rematch. The second encounter took place in November in New Orleans. This time, Leonard used his footwork to keep out of the champion's range, taunting him as he did so. In a move that shocked everyone who was watching, a frustrated Duran quit in the eighth round.

The contest would forever be known as the "No Mas" fight (the Spanish for "no more") although, despite reports to the contrary, Duran never actually said the words himself. The contest marked a turning point in

Roberto Duran (left) attacks Wilfred Benitez during the course of their 1982 world title fight. Duran lost the contest, one of several defeats during a low period in his career.

the fighter's life. Beforehand, he had been not only a national hero but a symbol of Latino machismo. He returned to his homeland an object of scorn and ridicule.

While the early section of his career, had been marked by almost universal success – the defeat against Leonard had been only his second in 74 fights – the later part would be characterized by a succession of highs and lows as humiliating defeats would be followed by heroic returns to form.

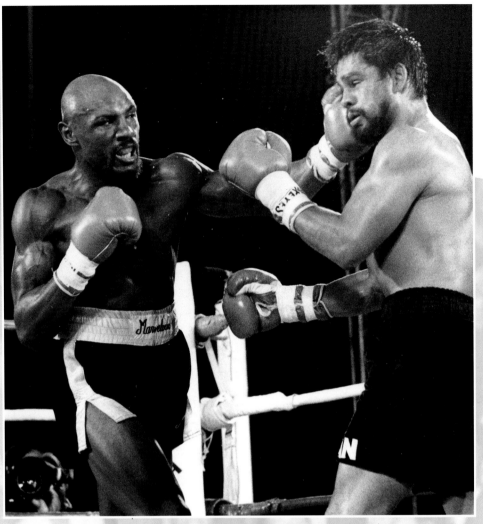

In 1983 Duran took on world middleweight champion Marvin Hagler (left). Duran failed in his attempt to add the middleweight crown to the light middleweight title that he already held.

Roberto Duran knocks Davey Moore to the canvas en route to an eighth-round win that would land him a world title in a third different weight class.

Duran responded to the Leonard loss by moving up in weight again, this time to junior middleweight (70kg or 154lb). After two successful warm-up fights in this new category, he challenged Wilfred Benitez for the world title in the division, but lost by unanimous decision. He was then beaten by Kirkland Laing, an unfancied fighter from the United Kingdom.

The loss to Laing left Duran less marketable than he had been for years, but a victory over Pipino Cuevas in January 1983 unexpectedly gave him a shot at Davey Moore's WBA junior middleweight title. In a stunning return to form, Duran overwhelmed the champion, forcing his corner to throw in the towel in the eighth round. Duran's success forced his name back into the spotlight and set him up for lucrative contests against two of the biggest names in the sport: Marvin Hagler and Thomas Hearns.

Duran met Hagler on 10 November 1983 at Caesar's Palace, Las Vegas. The middleweight champion Hagler was now at the peak of his powers. Despite the fact that both boxers had a reputation for ferocity in the ring, the contest turned out to be a relatively cautious affair. It was only in the final rounds that Hagler exerted his authority to win a narrow decision. In contrast to the Hagler fight, the contest with Hearns was an annihilation. For the first time in his career, Duran found himself completely overpowered. He was knocked down twice in the first round, and a third knockdown in the second brought the fight to a rapid conclusion.

Once again, Duran found his career on the rocks and once again he made an unlikely recovery. After the Hearns fight he stayed away from the ring for 18 months. He returned to competition in January 1986. A series of successful comeback fights over the course of the next three years led to a contest with Iran Barkley for the WBC middleweight title. By the time the fight took place in February 1989 Duran was 37 years old, but he

Thomas "the Hitman" Hearns (left) delivers a straight left to the face of Roberto Duran. Hearns overwhelmed Duran in just two rounds. It was the most comprehensive defeat of the Panamanian's 119-fight career.

somehow managed to summon up enough of his old strength, skill and courage to win a split decision.

The victory over Barkley proved to be Duran's last great fight. He followed it with a third contest with Leonard, a disappointing 12-round decision loss. Duran then stayed away from the ring for two years, before embarking on one of boxing's most protracted farewells. For over a decade Duran defied nature to continue to fight. His career was finally brought to an end not by a realization of his own fading powers but by fate. In October 2001 the fighter was involved in an car accident in Argentina. The injuries he sustained were sufficient to make a return to the ring impossible. Duran's final fight, a decision loss to Hector Camacho, had occurred just three months earlier, when he was 50 years old. He retired with a record of 103 wins in 119 contests.

Roberto Duran sends Iran Barkley to the canvas in 1989. In the last great performance of his career, Duran won a split decision to claim the world middleweight title.

In a match between two veterans, Roberto Duran took on Hector Camacho in 20 July 2001.

Roberto Duran's third fight with Sugar Ray Leonard came nine years after their first encounter. Here, Leonard lands a left to Duran's chin.

Larry Holmes

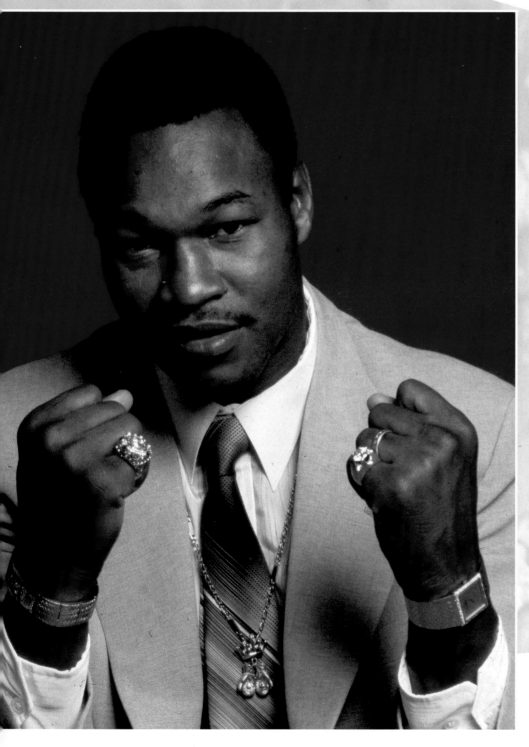

One of the least celebrated of boxing's great heavyweight champions, Larry Holmes ruled during a transitional period in the sport's history. The golden age of heavyweight boxing, when the exploits of Muhammad Ali, George Foreman and Joe Frazier captivated audiences across the globe, was over. The Tyson era was yet to come. However, in many ways, Holmes's record exceeds that of any of these more famous names. He was unbeaten for his first 48 fights and defended his title 20 times, a total bettered only by Joe Louis.

Larry Holmes was born on 3 November 1949, in Cuthbert, Georgia, but grew up in Easton, Pennsylvania, the town that would give him the nickname the "Easton Assassin". Holmes began boxing as a teenager, but like another great heavyweight champion, Rocky Marciano, had relatively little success in the amateur ranks. He finished with a record of 19 wins and three defeats, after failing to land a slot in the US team for the 1972 Olympics.

Holmes made his professional debut on 21 March 1973, when he defeated Rodell Dupree on points in Scranton, Pennsylvania. He continued to work his way up the professional ladder while simultaneously acting as a sparring partner for some of the biggest names in the sport. Joe Frazier employed him in the build-up to his January 1974 fight with Muhammad Ali. Later that year, Holmes trained with Ali, angering his employer with claims that he had proved the better fighter behind closed doors. They would eventually meet in public, but not before both their careers had undergone considerable transformations.

In 1975 Holmes parted company with Ali to concentrate on his own professional career. The "Easton Assassin" continued on his winning streak and by the beginning of 1978 had established himself as one of the leading contenders for the heavyweight crown. In an eliminator for the right to fight for the title, Holmes was pitched against Earnie Shavers, often cited as the

Larry Holmes holds up the fists that he used to defend the world heavyweight title 20 times. Holmes's reign lasted for more than seven years.

hardest puncher in the history of the sport. On this occasion, however, Shavers was comprehensively outboxed by Holmes and never got the opportunity to unleash his power. Holmes won a unanimous decision, setting up a confrontation with Ken Norton for the world heavyweight championship.

After winning the title from Ken Norton, Holmes defended the title three times before granting the hard-

hitting Earnie Shavers a rematch in September 1979. On this occasion, Shavers was able to land the big punch that had eluded him in their earlier encounter, sending Holmes to the canvas with a right hook in the seventh. The champion showed his resilience by dominating the remainder of the contest, landing countless heavy blows on a fatigued Shavers and forcing the referee to stop the contest in the 11th.

Larry Holmes (left) is struck by Earnie Shavers during Holmes's fourth defence of his world title. Shavers is universally recognized as one of the hardest punchers in the history of boxing.

HOLMES NORTON

In 1978 the heavyweight boxing picture became confused when Leon Spinks scored an unexpected victory against Muhammad Ali in a title clash in Las Vegas. The world had viewed the match as a routine defence for Ali before a more serious contest against number one contender Ken Norton. Spinks's decision to opt for a high-profile rematch against Ali rather than face Norton had prompted differing decisions from the sport's two governing bodies, the World Boxing Association (WBA) and World Boxing Council (WBC). While the WBA allowed Spinks to keep the title, the WBC stripped him, and handed the belt to Norton. For Norton, the WBC's decision was a rare stroke of fortune in a career beset by bad luck. In particular, he had been on the wrong end of an extremely debatable decision in his third fight against Ali in 1976, a fight that would have earned him the title.

Norton's first defence, set for 9 June 1978, would be against Larry Holmes. Like many great title fights, the contest revolved around a contrast of styles. Norton, the stronger puncher, wanted a close-quarter brawl, while Holmes preferred to fight at distance,

A straight right hand from heavyweight champion Ken Norton (right) catches Larry Holmes flush on the chin. The pair's 1978 title fight was Norton's first defence of his heavyweight crown.

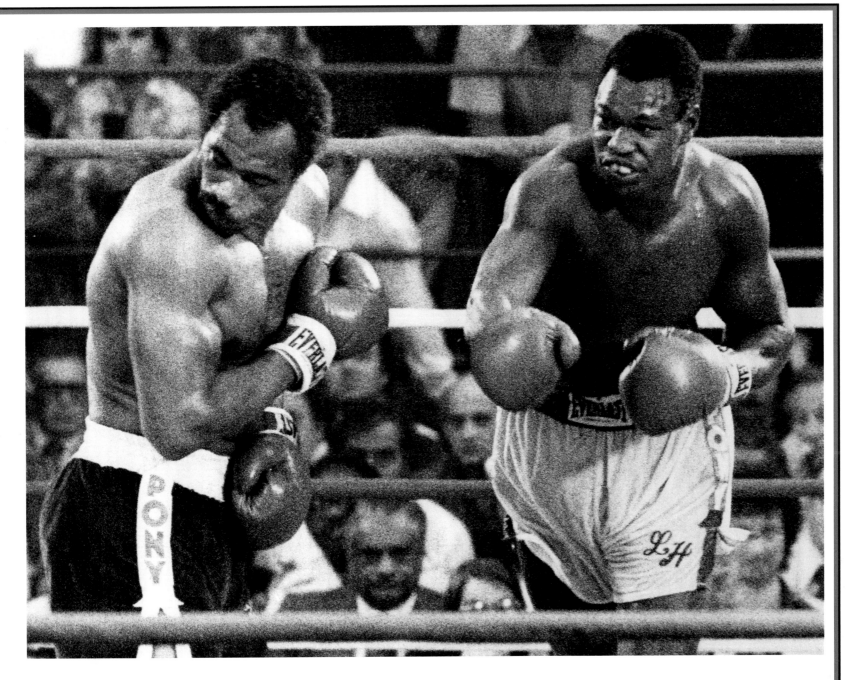

Larry Holmes (right) delivers a right hook to the jaw of Ken Norton. Holmes won the fight on a split decision, but only after a dramatic final round.

using his superior footwork to keep out of range. For the first six rounds, the fight followed Holmes's script, as he used his most potent weapon, a hard left jab, to keep Norton at bay. In the middle of the fight, however, the tide turned, and Norton managed to impose his style on the challenger.

By round 15, the contest was too close to call, with both boxers aware that the decision might go to whoever dominated the final three minutes. What followed was one of the greatest last rounds in heavyweight boxing history, as the two fighters exchanged ferocious punches in a desperate attempt to keep the outcome out of the hands of the judges. In the end, Holmes won by the narrowest of margins: one gave the fight to Norton by a single point, while the other two gave it to Holmes by the same margin. For Holmes, the contest would prove to be the beginning of a long and illustrious career at the top. For Norton, it was merely the beginning of the end. He fought just five more times, two of those matches resulting in first round defeats.

In 1980 Holmes continued his run of successful defences with comfortable wins over Lorenzo Zanon, Leroy Jones and Scott LeDoux before taking part in the most high-profile contest of his career, a fight against Muhammad Ali. The fight took place in Las Vegas on 2 October 1980, just over a year after Ali had announced his retirement. Because he had never lost his title in the ring, some fans still saw Ali as the true heavyweight champion. However, Ali was now almost 39 years old and already displaying symptoms of the neurological problems that would later paralyse him. For 10 rounds, while the crowd chanted "Ali! Ali!", Holmes hit the former champion at will. Eventually, Ali's

concerned trainer Angelo Dundee told the referee to stop the contest.

The win over Ali consolidated Holmes's position as the number one fighter in the world. He followed it up with a decision victory over Trevor Berbick and a third-round stoppage of Ali's former conqueror, Leon Spinks, before taking part in one of the biggest and most controversial contests of the decade. Holmes's opponent was Gerry Cooney, a big, undefeated Irish-American with a string of first-round knockouts to his name. In addition to his record, Cooney's other marketable asset was the colour of his skin. It had been 22 years since a white man had held the heavyweight championship of

Muhammad Ali (right) lands a rare punch during his 1980 fight with Larry Holmes. Holmes completely dominated the contest and spent much of it pummelling a nearly defenceless Ali.

Referee Richard Greene (right) walks away from Muhammad Ali's corner to inform Larry Holmes that he has won their fight. Ali's cornerman Angelo Dundee withdrew his fighter to prevent him from taking further punishment.

Gerry Cooney (right) collapses to the canvas during the 13th round of his world title fight with Larry Holmes. Controversially, publicity for the contest centred on the fight's racial dimension.

the world and the contest's promoters were happy to play up the racial dimension of the fight.

By the time the contest took place on 11 June 1982, tensions had been inflamed so much that both fighters had received death threats. Cooney had the backing of the majority of the crowd, but his supporters were rocked when Holmes knocked the challenger to the canvas in only the second round. Cooney recovered, but as the fight wore on, Holmes's greater technique and stamina started to prevail. Cooney hit the canvas again in the 11th and a further Holmes onslaught in the 13th prompted Cooney's corner to throw in the towel.

Holmes won five more fights before relinquishing the WBC heavyweight title for that of the newly formed International Boxing Federation (IBF). A further three victories over James "Bonecrusher" Smith, David Bey and Carl Williams brought him close to one of the most cherished statistics in the sport. Holmes's record now stood at 48 wins and no defeats, just one short of the 49-0 of Rocky Marciano.

Holmes's next opponent would be Michael Spinks, brother of former opponent Leon. Michael Spinks had won Olympic gold at middleweight before claiming the

world light heavyweight title as a professional. Spinks came into the fight more than 9kg (20lb) lighter than Holmes, and used his greater mobility and awkward style to frustrate the champion. Although Holmes was never seriously in trouble, the sheer number of punches landed by Spinks swayed the judges. Spinks was declared the new heavyweight champion.

The inevitable rematch was held on 19 April 1986. Holmes was much more aggressive than he had been in the pair's previous encounter, and at the end of the allotted 15 rounds, most observers believed that Holmes had done enough to regain his belt. Two of the three judges disagreed, however. A disgusted Holmes promptly retired.

Like many of boxing's great champions, Holmes did not stay retired for long. His first return to the ring came in January 1988 when he accepted a lucrative offer to face the new undisputed champion, Mike Tyson. The fight had sad echoes of Holmes's own demolition of Ali just over seven years earlier.

Holmes's well-honed defensive skills allowed him to survive for three rounds, but in round four Tyson launched a series of savage attacks to knock Holmes down three times. The referee had no choice but to stop the contest.

The nature of the defeat against Tyson persuaded Holmes to stay away from boxing for three years, but he eventually returned at age 41 to pursue an unlikely

In 1988, Larry Holmes came out of retirement to face the seemingly invincible new champion Mike Tyson (right). Holmes could not compete with the younger man, and lost in four rounds.

second career that gave him three further shots at versions of the heavyweight title. A surprise win against former Olympic champion Ray Mercer in 1992 set up a fight with champion Evander Holyfield. Holyfield won comfortably on points, but Holmes persevered. After a series of wins against journeymen opponents, he was rewarded with a fight against WBC champion Oliver McCall. Victory would have made the 45-year-old Holmes the oldest ever heavyweight champion, but the judges awarded McCall a narrow decision.

Still undeterred, Holmes carried on. Nominally at least, he fought once more for the world title, a split-decision loss to the Dane Brian Nielsen, but this was for the International Boxing Organization (IBO) crown, a minor title that was not recognized by most boxing observers. His final contest was a 2002 win over Eric Esch, an overweight, crowd-pleasing fighter known to his fans as "Butterbean". By this time Holmes was 52 years old. He then retired to concentrate on his numerous business interests.

Larry Holmes's final opponent was Eric "Butterbean" Esch (left), a boxer mainly known for his bloated physique. Even though he was 52 years old, Holmes still won comfortably.

Marvin Hagler

Marvin Hagler dominated the middleweight division in the 1980s. He held the world title for more than six years and became one of the most recognizable faces in the sport. The road to the top was a long one, however. Hagler toiled away on obscure cards for years, only fighting for the title in his 50th contest. Even then, he would be denied by a controversial decision.

Marvin Nathaniel Hagler was born in Newark, New Jersey on 23 May 1954, but moved to Brockton, Massachusetts as a child, a relocation prompted largely by the riots that tore Newark apart in 1967. Hagler took up boxing at age 16 when a beating in a street fight persuaded him to check out the nearby Petronelli Brothers' Gym. Hagler would remain loyal to the Petronellis for the rest of his career.

Under the Petronellis' guidance, Hagler progressed quickly. A successful amateur career reached a climax in 1973 when Hagler won the National Amateur Athletic Union crown. A prestigious title such as this was seen as an indication of Olympic potential, but the Montreal games were still three years away and Hagler chose instead to turn professional. The move was prompted by financial necessity: the boxer had recently married and become a father.

Hagler made his professional debut against Terry Ryan on 18 May 1973, winning by a second-round knockout. By this point, he had already adopted a look and a nickname that would stay with him until the end of his career. Hagler had first started shaving his head as an amateur in the hope that the move might help blows glance off his head, but kept the look as a trademark. He had also added an adjective to his name: he was now "Marvelous" Marvin Hagler.

For the first 18 months of his career, most of Hagler's fights took place in Massachusetts. His opponents were

Marvin Hagler poses for the cameras in 1977. By this time Hagler had built up a reputation as a dangerous middleweight, but had not yet been given a title shot.

Marvin Hagler (right) launches an attack on Sugar Ray Seales in the first of their two encounters. Seales was one of the most dangerous of Hagler's early opponents.

Marvin Hagler (right) ducks under a punch from Vito Antuofermo during the course of their 1979 world title fight. The contest ended in a controversial draw.

Marvin Hagler and his entourage shelter from a hail of cans and bottles after Hagler's victory over Englishman Alan Minter. The win earned Hagler the world middleweight championship.

either fellow novices or journeymen and few tested him seriously. Hagler's first major fight came in August 1974 when he took on Sugar Ray Seales, a gold medallist at the 1972 Olympic Games. Both fighters had perfect professional records – Hagler had 14 wins to Seales' 21 – but Hagler prevailed to mark himself out as a fighter to be watched.

Hagler's managers often found it difficult to find him fights against other up-and-coming prospects. His talent was only part of the problem. Hagler fought out of the southpaw stance usually favoured by left-handers. However, he was actually right-handed and could switch to an orthodox stance whenever he needed to and this awkward style gave him a reputation as an opponent to be avoided.

By the end of 1975 Hagler was still undefeated, the only blemish in his 26 fights being a draw in a rematch with Seales. The following year began badly, however. By the middle of March he had suffered two defeats, both in Philadelphia and both against local fighters: Bobby Watts and Willie "the Worm" Monroe. The losses left Hagler's career at a dangerous junction, but he soon rallied, beating another dangerous fighter from Philadelphia, Eugene Hart, and then twice avenging his loss against Monroe.

Tony Sibson (left) lands a hard left to the face of Marvin Hagler. Hagler went on to win their 1983 fight in the sixth round.

Hagler continued to be successful inside the ring, but a lack of connections still prevented him from competing for the world middleweight title. The perceived injustice was so great that the influential Massachusetts senator Ted Kennedy put his weight behind a campaign for Hagler to get a title shot.

Eventually such pressure paid off, and on 30 November 1979 Hagler fought the Italian-American Vito Antuofermo for the middleweight crown. The contest took place on the undercard of Sugar Ray Leonard's attempt to wrest the welterweight title from Wilfred Benitez. Hagler began the fight strongly, but despite his superior boxing ability was unable to put the rugged Antuofermo away. At the end of the 15 rounds, Hagler clearly believed he had done enough to win the title. One judge agreed. However, another gave it to Antuofermo, while the third scored it a draw.

Hagler would get a chance to avenge himself, but not until after he had won the world championship. After his surprise draw with Hagler – the challenger had been the favourite for the contest – Antuofermo promptly lost his title to Englishman Alan Minter in Las Vegas. Antuofermo also lost the rematch in London, paving the way for a title clash between Minter and Hagler in autumn 1980.

Hagler met Minter in front of a charged and partisan crowd at Wembley, London, on 27 September 1980, the atmosphere inflamed by Minter's pre-fight comment that "no black man" was going to take his title away. After the Antuofermo fight, Hagler was keen not to leave the outcome to the judges and began the fight aggressively. Minter was tough and talented, but prone to cuts and it was not long before blood was dripping from his face. By the middle of the third round the

HAGLER

HEARNS

Tommy Hearns and Marvin Hagler had been potential rivals for several years before they finally touched gloves on 15 April 1985. Fighting out of the Kronk gym in Detroit, Hearns had begun his professional career as a welterweight, fighting at 67kg (147lb). At 1.85m (6ft 1in), he was extremely tall for his weight and incredibly powerful, winning 30 of his first 32 fights inside the distance. He eventually won the division's

world title, but after losing it to Sugar Ray Leonard, moved up to light middleweight (70kg or 154lb), where he again became world champion. His fight against Hagler would see him attempting to win a title in a third weight class.

Marvin Hagler (left) and Thomas Hearns exchange punches during their short and explosive encounter in Las Vegas in 1985. Hagler recovered from a bad cut to win in three rounds.

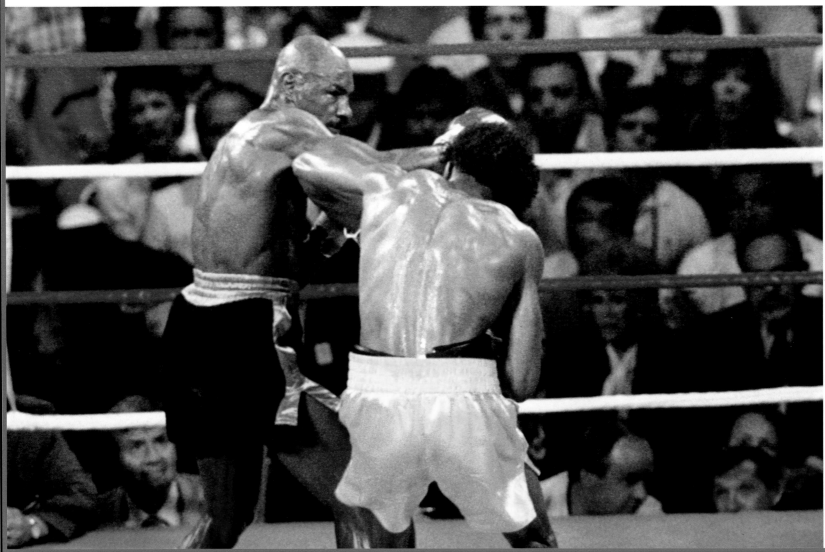

*Thomas Hearns lies sprawled on the canvas
after being knocked out by Marvin Hagler
in their world title fight.*

Billed simply as "The Fight", the showdown between Hagler and Hearns took place at Caesar's Palace, Las Vegas. Public interest, which was already huge, had been heightened by a lengthy build-up in which the two fighters had travelled the country exchanging insults. The opening exchanges suggested that the vitriol may have been genuine. The start of the first round saw both fighters launch reckless all-out assaults. Neither man was prepared to back down and the intensity continued for the full three minutes.

The frenetic pace continued in round two, with Hagler getting slightly the better of the action. By now, however, both men were injured. Hearns had broken his hand, while Hagler was badly cut. Although Hearns's injury was the more serious of the two,

Hagler's presented the greater immediate danger. After a minute of the third round, the referee stopped the bout so that the cut could be examined. The contest was waved on, but Hagler knew that a second intervention might bring the bout to a conclusion and fought accordingly. Within a minute, another full-blown assault from Hagler had left Hearns sprawled on the canvas. The contest was over.

The fight between Hagler and Hearns had lasted less than eight minutes, but would go down as one of the most memorable in history. It would prove the climax of Hagler's career. Hearns had now lost two of the biggest fights of the decade, but would go on to become the first man to win world titles at five different weights.

Marvin Hagler (right) prepares to punch Roberto Duran in the first round of their fight in 1983. Hagler won in 15 rounds to retain his middleweight title.

damage was so great that the referee stopped the contest, prompting a hail of beer cans to rain into the ring. Hagler had won the title, but would be escorted from the ring under a police escort before he could be awarded his belt.

The victory over Minter marked the start of a six-and-a-half-year reign as middleweight champion. Hagler's first defence came against the unbeaten Venezuelan Fulgencio Obelmejias, who was dispatched in the eighth round. The champion then fought a rematch against Vito Antuofermo. This time, the contest only made it to the beginning of the fifth round, when cuts forced the Italian-American's corner to throw in the towel.

Hagler continued to defend his title against a series of tough challengers such as Mustafa Hamsho, William "Caveman" Lee and Tony Sibson, before facing the current junior middleweight champion Roberto Duran on 10 November 1983. Duran was now in his 16th year as a professional and fighting above his natural weight, but still proved a difficult opponent, cutting the champion in the later part of the contest. The damage prompted Hagler to push the action in the last two rounds to seal a close decision victory.

After the contest with Duran, Hagler began to fight less frequently. He competed just twice in 1984 and once in 1985, a short but brutal contest with Tommy Hearns that would prove his most famous victory. The win against Hearns was followed up by a contest with the unbeaten Ugandan John "the Beast" Mugabi. Mugabi proved to be a more resilient opponent than many observers had predicted, but Hagler still managed to knock him out in the 11th round.

The victory over Mugabi in March 1986 left Hagler with one obvious opponent – the only problem was that he was officially retired. The former welterweight champion Sugar Ray Leonard had not fought since 1984, but watching Hagler's defence against Mugabi had convinced him that he could defeat the champion. A challenge was issued and eventually accepted, and the fight arranged for 6 April 1987.

Because of Leonard's lengthy lay-off from boxing, Hagler entered the ring confident of victory, but was frustrated by his opponent's tactics. Leonard fought on the retreat, catching Hagler with isolated flurries of punches, before dancing out of reach. As the fight wore on, Hagler began to impose himself, but the pattern remained the same; Hagler landed the harder punches, Leonard the showier ones. In the end, one of the judges scored it for Hagler, two for Leonard. The decision would be a subject of debate for years to come.

After the Leonard fight, a disgusted Hagler retired from boxing altogether, and unlike many of his contemporaries, refused to be tempted out of retirement in later life. He subsequently moved to Italy, where he continued to be recognized as one of the greatest middleweights of all time.

Marvin Hagler's career ended in controversial and disappointing fashion when Sugar Ray Leonard (left) beat him by way of split decision in 1987. Hagler was convinced that he had won the fight.

Sugar Ray Leonard

More than almost any other boxer, Sugar Ray Leonard seemed destined for greatness from his first professional contest. By the time Leonard entered the paid ranks, he was already a star, the most high profile of five US boxers to win gold medals at the 1976 Olympic Games. Television networks and promoters were keen to play up his good looks and wholesome image, yet Leonard repeatedly proved that beneath this veneer he could be as tough and resilient as any of his contemporaries.

Ray Charles Leonard was born on 17 May 1956 in Wilmington, North Carolina. As a child he moved first to Washington DC and then to Palmer Park, Maryland. Although his family was by no means rich, Leonard did not experience the kind of grinding poverty that served as an incentive for many other great champions. He learned to box at the Palmer Park Recreation Center, where he and his fellow young fighters trained in a makeshift ring marked out by tape on a basketball court. The lack of professional facilities did not hamper Leonard's progress. In 1972 he won the National Golden Gloves title at lightweight. He repeated the feat the following year, before winning the junior welterweight title in 1974. The same year, he also won the Amateur Athletic Union title at the same weight.

By the time of the 1976 Olympic Games in Montreal, Leonard's reputation had spread and his contests were televized from the start of the competition. Five straight wins earned Leonard an appearance in the final against Cuban southpaw Andres Aldama. Leonard began by circling away from his opponent's stronger left hand, but as he grew more confident he started to engage in close-quarter exchanges. Standing counts for the Cuban in both the second and third rounds rendered the judges' decision a formality. Leonard had crowned his amateur career with an Olympic gold medal.

By winning an Olympic title, Leonard had joined an elite group of US boxers that included three of the

Sugar Ray Leonard relaxes in front of a poster for his 1978 clash with Dickie Ecklund. Even at this early stage of his career, Leonard was already a star.

Trainer Angelo Dundee gives instructions to Sugar Ray Leonard during a sparring session. Dundee was in Leonard's corner from the early days of his professional career.

Pete Ranzany (left) looks on after throwing a punch at a teenage Sugar Ray Leonard in an amateur contest in 1973.

biggest names in the sport – Muhammad Ali, George Foreman and Joe Frazier. The most obvious next step for Leonard was a move to the professional game, where his Olympic success would guarantee immediate financial returns. The boxer himself, however, was adamant that he would make no such move. On returning to Washington he told a crowd of well-wishers: "This medal is all I ever wanted. I will never be a professional fighter." This was the first time that Leonard would retire, but by no means the last.

Leonard's plan was to enrol at the University of Maryland, where his living expenses would be covered

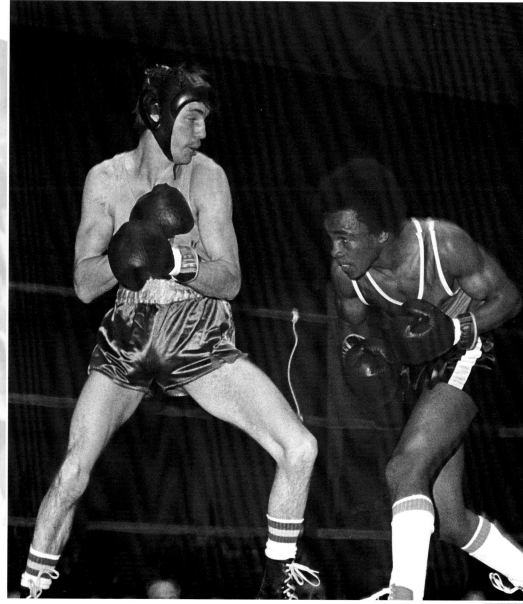

LEONARD DURAN II

The fight between Sugar Ray Leonard and Roberto Duran in Montreal had been a classic, a closely contested war that could have been won by either boxer. Like many sequels, the rematch was in some ways a disappointment. It featured few of the thrilling exchanges of the previous contest. However, it would become even more famous than its predecessor.

The Leonard camp's post mortem into their fighter's defeat in the first Duran fight did not reveal anything that was not apparent to most seasoned observers in the crowd: Sugar Ray had lost because he had fought Duran's fight rather than his own. For personal psychological reasons, he had set out to prove that he was capable of outbrawling Duran as well as outboxing him.

Sugar Ray Leonard (right) taunts Roberto Duran by inviting him to hit his chin. Leonard used tactics such as this throughout the pair's 1980 rematch.

Roberto Duran (left) quits in the middle of his fight with Sugar Ray Leonard. A shocked Leonard raises his hands in celebration.

The fact that he had failed so narrowly convinced Leonard that he could win a rematch.

The return encounter took place at the New Orleans Superdome on 25 November 1980, just five months after the first contest. The short interval was a calculated move on the part of the Leonard team, who knew that Duran's wild post-fight celebrations often caused him to balloon up in size. Duran had indeed put on weight in the period between the two fights, but his problems would be psychological rather than physical.

For the first six rounds, Leonard used his superior footwork to stay out of Duran's reach, catching the Panamanian with enough shots to build up a comfortable though not overwhelming lead. The tactics clearly frustrated Duran, and in the seventh, Leonard began to openly taunt his opponent, sticking out his chin and daring Duran to hit it. The move had an even greater effect than Leonard could have imagined. In the following round, Duran simply turned his back on Leonard and quit.

Duran's actions would never be satisfactorily explained. The official reason offered by his camp was that he was suffering from stomach cramps, yet few observers believed this to be the case. A more popular theory was that his pride would not allow him to be humiliated. Whatever the reason, Duran's refusal to continue led to him being ridiculed. Despite an illustrious career that would encompass more than 100 victories and world titles at four separate weights, Duran's name would forever be associated with two words: "no mas", Spanish for "no more".

lightweight champion Roberto Duran. The fight, which became known as the "Brawl in Montreal", took Leonard back to the site of his Olympic success. From a promoter's viewpoint the matchup was perfect. It pitched Leonard's clean-cut boy next door against Duran's scowling street fighter. The two boxers' fighting styles also stood in clear contrast to one another. While the stylish boxer Leonard used his footwork to keep out of range, Duran was a rugged brawler who liked to trade punches at close quarters.

When the two boxers stepped into the ring at the Olympic Stadium on 20 June 1980, the crowd was treated to a very different kind of a fight to the one that they were expecting. Rather than playing the matador to Duran's bull, Leonard elected to stand toe-to-toe with the Panamanian for all 15 rounds. The unexpected tactics almost paid off. After being dominated in the early rounds, Leonard sprung to life in the fifth and sixth, and from this moment onward the fight appeared too close to call. In the end, however, the judges awarded a narrow victory to Duran. A rematch was inevitable.

Leonard followed his two confrontations with Duran with victories over Larry Bonds and Ayub Kalule. These wins set up a showdown with Tommy Hearns to unify the two world welterweight crowns: Hearns held the WBA version of the title, Leonard its WBC equivalent. The fight, which took place at Caesar's Palace, Las Vegas, on 16 September 1981, was one of fluctuating fortunes. Leonard initially found himself outboxed, but came back strongly in the sixth and seventh rounds. Hearns then reasserted himself and by the beginning of the 13th round, Leonard needed a knockout for victory. Urged on by Angelo Dundee, he immediately went on the attack and twice knocked Hearns through the ropes. Only the bell saved Hearns, and further onslaughts in the 14th forced the referee to stop the contest.

The following year, Leonard fought Bruce Finch in what should have been a routine defence of his title. In one way it was routine – Leonard won by technical knockout in the third round. However, a medical held after the fight showed that Leonard had suffered a detached retina. An operation fixed the problem, but after several months' deliberation, Leonard retired.

Thomas Hearns slumps into the ropes in the 14th round of his 1981 title fight with Sugar Ray Leonard. Referee Davey Pearl prepares to step in to save him.

Sugar Ray Leonard (right) knocks out Donny Lalonde to win world titles in a fourth and fifth weight class.

From this moment on, Leonard's career would be marked by a series of short-lived comebacks and subsequent retirements. His first return came in May 1984, when he defeated Kevin Howard in nine rounds and, dissatisfied with his lacklustre performance, quit immediately afterwards. He stayed away from the ring for almost three years, but was tempted back to fight Marvin Hagler for the middleweight title.

By the time that Leonard faced him on 6 April 1987, Hagler had been champion for six and a half years.

Many questioned the wisdom of Leonard's return. His lengthy lay-off combined with Hagler's natural size advantage meant that he went into the fight as clear underdog. Strategically, however, Leonard fought a perfect fight. He used his superior mobility to keep tantalizingly out of range and scored with just enough shots to claim a narrow victory.

For his next contest, Leonard would step up in weight once again to fight the Canadian Donny Lalonde, the WBC champion at light heavyweight (79kg or 175lb).

Hector Camacho (right) hits Sugar Ray Leonard with a right hand during Leonard's final fight. Camacho won by a fifth-round technical knockout.

An arrangement was made whereby the fight would be held at 76kg (168lb) so that two titles could be at stake – the light heavyweight crown and that for the newly created super middleweight (76kg or 168lb) division. Although he was forced to the canvas early on, Leonard recovered to win by stoppage in the ninth.

Leonard had now won world titles at five different weights, an almost unprecedented achievement. Only one man had achieved the feat before. That man was Tommy Hearns, and he had done so just three days previously. The two boxers' parallel achievements made a rematch between them inevitable and they duly met at Caesar's Palace on 12 June 1989. As had been the case in their 1981 encounter, there was little to choose between the two fighters. This time, however, there would be no dramatic late stoppage by Leonard, and the judges scored the contest a draw.

Leonard now turned to another former opponent, Roberto Duran. The third contest between the pair provided neither the all-out ferocity of the first encounter nor the dramatic ending of the second. Leonard fought a cautious but effective fight to win a comfortable decision.

Like many great champions, Leonard sullied his legacy by continuing to fight when past his prime. In 1991 he returned to the ring to be easily beaten by junior welterweight champion Terry Norris, who was more than 11 years younger than him. Then, after a further lay-off of six years, he lost by technical knockout to Hector Camacho. It was the only stoppage loss of Leonard's professional career and persuaded him to retire for good.

After his ring career had ended, Leonard dabbled in acting and boxing promotion, but his most high-profile public role came with his involvement in the reality TV show *The Contender*, in which journeymen boxers competed to win a lucrative professional contract. Leonard presented the first three series of the programme, which ran from 2005 to 2007.

Sugar Ray Leonard addresses the crowd during the recording of an episode of the reality TV series The Contender. *The show gave journeymen boxers a chance to achieve stardom.*

Mike Tyson

Mike Tyson (right) throws a punch at Marvis Frazier, the son of former heavyweight champion Joe Frazier, in July, 1986. Like many of Tyson's early opponents, Frazier only lasted a single round.

Mike Tyson was both boxing's youngest-ever heavyweight champion and its most brutally destructive. In the late 1980s he injected new life into a moribund heavyweight division, unifying its various titles with a series of electrifying performances. In the process, Tyson secured the fascination of not just the boxing fraternity, but also the public at large. However, while his rise was brief and spectacular, Tyson's fall from grace was long, ignominious and very public.

Michael Gerard Tyson was born in Brooklyn, New York, on 30 June 1966. Tyson was relatively shy while a young child, but from age eight onwards he gradually became dragged into the brutal gang culture that characterized life in the low-income neighbourhood of Brownsville at that time. His continued involvement in street fights and robbery eventually led to his incarceration in the Tryon Reform School in New York State. It was here that Tyson was introduced to boxing.

The institution's athletic coach was Bobby Stewart, a welterweight boxer who spotted Tyson's potential after sparring with him, the first time that the 12-year-old had laced on gloves. Stewart brought Tyson to the attention of Cus D'Amato, a veteran boxing coach who had worked with former world heavyweight champion Floyd Patterson. Almost immediately, D'Amato became convinced that Tyson could replicate Patterson's achievement. He persuaded the authorities to allow Tyson to move in with his family in Catskill, where he supervised the young boxer's training.

Although he won a National Golden Gloves championship in 1984, Tyson's aggressive style was

Trevor Berbick (left) flinches from an onslaught by Mike Tyson during the course of their bout in November, 1986. Tyson's win made him the youngest-ever world heavyweight champion.

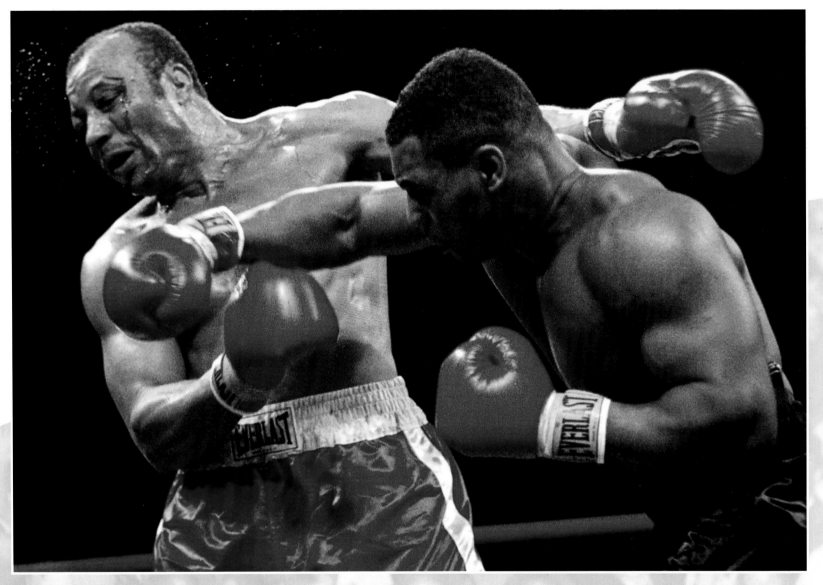

Mike Tyson (right) lands a right hand to the jaw of James "Bonecrusher" Smith. Tyson went on to win the fight by decision, adding the WBA heavyweight title to the WBC crown that he already held.

more suited to the professional than the amateur game. He made his paid debut on 6 March 1985, when he knocked out Hector Mercedes in one round. Over the course of the year, Tyson scored a further 14 victories, 10 of them coming in the first round. However, his successes in the ring were overshadowed by personal tragedy. In November, D'Amato died from pneumonia. The loss of his mentor had an enormous emotional impact on the young fighter.

With Kevin Rooney taking over D'Amato's duties as chief trainer, Tyson continued his winning streak. The quality of opposition changed, but the results did not, as seasoned veterans such as James Tillis and Marvis Frazier were unable to halt the young fighter's rise.

At only 1.78m (5ft 10in), "Iron" Mike was relatively small, but was extremely powerful and possessed incredible hand speed for a heavyweight. No one seemed to be able to withstand him, and a clamour inevitably grew for him to get a shot at one of the world heavyweight champions.

On 22 November 1986, Tyson received his first chance at a title when he faced the World Boxing Council (WBC) champion Trevor Berbick. Best known as the man who had ended the career of Muhammad Ali, the Canadian was vastly more experienced, having begun his professional ring career more than 10 years earlier. However, any spectators expecting a close contest would be disappointed, as Berbick was

TYSON SPINKS

Between November 1986, when he first claimed a portion of the heavyweight championship, and February 1990, when he lost his titles to James "Buster" Douglas, Mike Tyson treated the boxing public to a succession of devastating performances. While it is open to debate which one of these fights represented Tyson's peak as a fighter, his destruction of Michael Spinks on 27 June 1988 is a particularly strong candidate.

In the space of one year, Tyson had unified the previously fragmented heavyweight division by claiming the WBA, WBC and IBF belts. However, one slightly more vague title evaded him, that of linear champion. The linear championship, much loved by boxing historians, belonged to "the man who beat the man who beat the man". The concept harked back to a simpler age of boxing, when there was only one heavyweight champion and every man on the street knew who he was. By 1988, the title was in the hands of Michael Spinks, who had beaten Larry Holmes, the conqueror of Muhammad Ali.

A former Olympic champion who was unbeaten as a professional, Michael Spinks was superficially a formidable opponent. However, he had spent most of his career as a light heavyweight (79kg or 175lb) and had only fought four times at the upper level. The potential discrepancy in power between the two men seemed to occupy Spinks's mind and Tyson later said that he could sense fear in his opponent as soon as he saw his eyes.

The fight would be one of the shortest and most one-sided in heavyweight championship history. The first knockdown came through a Tyson body shot just over a minute into the contest. Spinks rose, only to be knocked out by the next combination that Tyson threw. The whole fight had lasted just 91 seconds.

Spinks took the contest as a signal that he should retire and never fought again. For Tyson, it was a high-water mark that added a new chapter to his legend and left boxing observers openly wondering if there was a heavyweight who was even capable of providing a challenge to him. Tyson's time at the top, however, would be briefer than they could imagine.

Michael Spinks (left) crumples to the canvas just a minute and a half into his title fight with Mike Tyson. Tyson put on one of his most dominant performances.

completely unable to withstand the younger man's power. The disparity became clear in the first round when a hook from Tyson sent Berbick staggering towards the ropes. The champion was forced to endure more punishment in the second as he was clubbed unceremoniously around the ring. The fight ended in spectacular fashion as another Tyson hook forced Berbick to the floor. The champion twice attempted to rise, only to collapse in tragicomic fashion. When he finally got to his feet, the referee stopped the contest. At 20 years and four months, Mike Tyson had become the youngest-ever heavyweight champion of the world.

Tyson would rule the heavyweight division for the next three years, as a succession of respected fighters failed to halt his progress. Most, but not all, were brushed aside in a similar manner to Berbick. Tyson's next opponent, the World Boxing Association (WBA) champion James "Bonecrusher" Smith managed to last the distance, but only by holding extensively, while former champion Pinklon Thomas was badly beaten for six rounds before being knocked out. Tyson then faced the International Boxing Federation (IBF) champion Tony Tucker in a bout that would unify the three versions of the world heavyweight title. Tucker presented Tyson

Former champion Larry Holmes (right) was unable to halt the rise of Mike Tyson. Holmes survived until the fourth round, but was then knocked unconscious by a right hook.

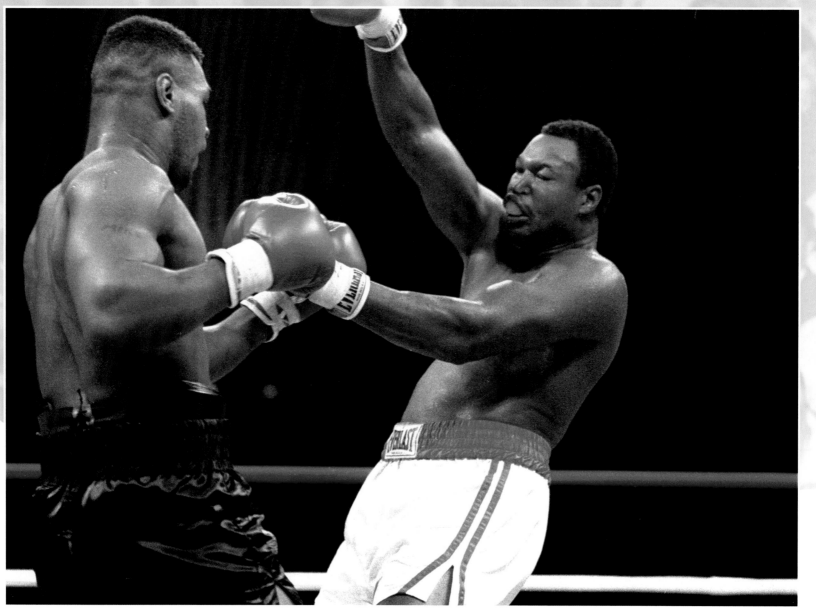

with the stiffest challenge of his career, hurting him early on, but at the end of the 12 rounds, the judges gave Tyson a clear decision victory. In October, the champion completed a successful year with a fourth defence of his title, a seventh-round stoppage of Tyrell Biggs.

Tyson's dominant form in 1987 prompted a search for worthy opponents. The great Larry Holmes was lured out of retirement in January 1988, but, out-of-shape and unprepared, lasted only four rounds. Tony Tubbs survived just two rounds in a clash held in Tokyo two months later. In June, meanwhile, Michael Spinks became the third former champion to be defeated by Tyson in the space of six months.

The champion's ring successes continued into the following year – Frank Bruno and Carl Williams were both beaten easily – but outside the ring, Tyson's life was spiralling out of control. His volatile marriage to the actress Robin Givens, barely a year old, was disintegrating. Behind the scenes, various management factions were engaged in a vicious fight to control his career. Prone to violent mood swings, the fighter had begun to take antidepressants.

James Douglas stands over a spread-eagled Mike Tyson after knocking him down in the 10th round of their 1990 title fight. Douglas's defeat of Tyson was one of the biggest upsets in the history of boxing.

Despite this chaos, Tyson went into his February 1990 bout with James "Buster" Douglas as overwhelming favourite. While many of Tyson's previous opponents had once been champions themselves, Douglas was a solid professional and no more. However, the underdog raised his game to hitherto unseen levels, utilizing a strong jab to control early sections of the fight. Tyson was almost saved when an uppercut at the end of round eight put Douglas on the floor. However, by the time that he rose on the count of nine, the round was over. Douglas showed few adverse effects in the ninth and upped the pressure in the 10th. Then, in a move that stunned the world of boxing, he knocked Tyson out with a perfectly executed combination of punches.

Tyson recovered from his loss with two first-round wins before the end of the year, the first coming against Henry Tillman, the second against Alex Stewart. Then in 1991 he twice defeated the hard-hitting Canadian Donovan Ruddock. The two victories set up an obvious and lucrative showdown with former cruiserweight (91kg or 200lb) champion Evander Holyfield, who had taken the unified championship from Douglas in the latter's first defence. However, in July 1991 Tyson was charged with raping Desiree Washington, a contestant in the Miss Black America beauty pageant. The fighter claimed that she had consented to sex, but when the case came to court in February 1992, the jury decided otherwise. Tyson was sentenced to six years in jail.

Six years after losing his heavyweight title to James Douglas, Mike Tyson reclaimed a portion of the crown by defeating British fighter Frank Bruno (left).

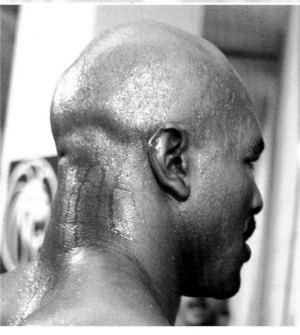

In fact, Tyson served just three years of his sentence. When he was released in March 1995, he emerged to find that his public profile had, if anything, increased during his incarceration. His first fight, a mismatch against journeyman Pete McNeeley, was promoted as "the biggest sporting event in the history of the world". It ended in the first round when McNeeley's cornerman came into the ring to get the referee to halt the contest. The official result was a disqualification victory for Tyson.

After one more warm-up fight, an easy win over Buster Mathis Jr, Tyson took on former opponent Frank Bruno for the WBC heavyweight crown. The British boxer, making the first defence of his title, was unable to make much more of an impression than he had in his first fight, and was stopped in three rounds. A second title bout, against WBA champion Bruce Seldon, was even shorter. Seldon was knocked down twice before the fight was stopped just within its second minute.

Mike Tyson prepares to rise after being knocked down in his first fight against Evander Holyfield. Holyfield went on to win in the 11th round.

The damage to Evander Holyfield's ear is clearly visible as he heads to the dressing room following his second fight with Mike Tyson. Tyson was disqualified for biting.

119

The Seldon fight set the scene for the encounter that had been slated to take place in the autumn of 1991. On 9 November 1996, Tyson fought Evander Holyfield at the MGM Grand in Las Vegas. Tyson entered the contest as overwhelming favourite on account of his greater natural size and some poor recent performances by the challenger. However, Holyfield fought the fight of his life, dominating his opponent to win by stoppage in the 11th round.

The rematch, which took place seven months later, would go down as one of the most extraordinary fights in history. While professional boxing has seen its share of dirty contests, seasoned onlookers were still shocked by the bout's climax. The first round passed uneventfully enough, but in the second, a headbutt from Holyfield opened up a cut above Tyson's right eye. Further use of the head by the challenger, either intentional or unintentional, infuriated Tyson, and in the third round he

Lennox Lewis (left) delivers a blow to the head of Mike Tyson during the first round of their contest in 2002. Lewis dominated the fight, stopping Tyson in the eighth round.

In 2003 Mike Tyson chose to have his face tattooed shortly before a fight. The decision was seen as an example of his increasingly unconventional behaviour.

got his revenge. Shortly before the end of the round, he bit a small chunk from Holyfield's right ear. The fight was stopped amid confusion, with two points deducted from Tyson. However, upon the restart, Tyson bit Holyfield once again. The inevitable disqualification prompted a brawl in the ring.

Tyson's actions led to a suspension, but one that was surprisingly brief. He returned to the ring just over 18 months later and, over the course of the next three years, worked his way through a series of overmatched opponents. However, this period of his life was more notable for problems out of the ring. He served another jail sentence – for assault – and he also continued to battle depression.

Tyson's final significant fight came on 8 June 2002 when he came up against the British/Canadian fighter Lennox Lewis, generally regarded as the best of the various heavyweight title holders. Taller and considerably heavier, Lewis controlled the early rounds with his jab before knocking Tyson out in the eighth. The build-up and aftermath to the contest exemplified the contradictory facets of Tyson's character. Before the bout he had threatened to eat Lewis's babies. Afterwards, he was polite, dignified and respectful, congratulating his conqueror on his performance.

After the defeat to Lewis, Tyson fought just three more times. A one-round knockout of Clifford Etienne was followed by shock defeats against Danny Williams and Kevin McBride. Aware that his powers were rapidly fading, Tyson called time on a professional career that had lasted more than 20 years. For three of those years at least, Tyson had lit up the sport like few before him.

Mike Tyson slumps against the ropes at the end of the final fight of his career. His opponent, Kevin McBride, walks back to his corner.

Roy Jones Jr

When he was at the height of his powers in the mid-1990s, Roy Jones Jr was widely regarded as pound-for-pound the best fighter in the world. An incredibly skilful boxer who possessed dazzling hand speed and astonishing reflexes, he would eventually win world titles in four separate weight divisions.

Roy Levesta Jones was born in Pensacola, Florida, on 16 January 1969. His introduction to boxing came courtesy of his father, Roy Jones Sr, who fashioned a makeshift gym for his son on the farm that he owned. By age 10, he was fighting competitively, the beginning of an illustrious amateur career. In 1986 Jones won the National Golden Gloves title at junior welterweight. A year later he claimed the equivalent title at junior middleweight. A third success eluded him when he lost to future world champion Gerald McClellan at the semifinal stage of the 1988 tournament, but victory in the Olympic trials presented him with an opportunity to claim the biggest prize in the amateur version of the sport.

When Jones arrived in Seoul for the 1988 Olympic Games, he was well aware that the events of the next few weeks would shape the rest of his professional career. What he could never have envisaged was that the result of one of his fights would have profound implications for the sport as a whole. Comfortable victories in Jones's first four bouts led to a place in the final against the South Korean Park Si-Hun. Jones dominated the contest, completely outclassing his opponent. However, at the end of the bout, three of the five judges awarded the fight to the hometown boxer.

While controversial decisions have always been a fixture of both professional and amateur boxing, the extent of this particular injustice led to an international outcry. Later analysis of the fight revealed that Jones had landed almost three times as many punches as his

Roy Jones Jr is pictured shortly after his 2002 win against Clinton Woods. Jones carries or wears three of the six world championship belts he held at the time.

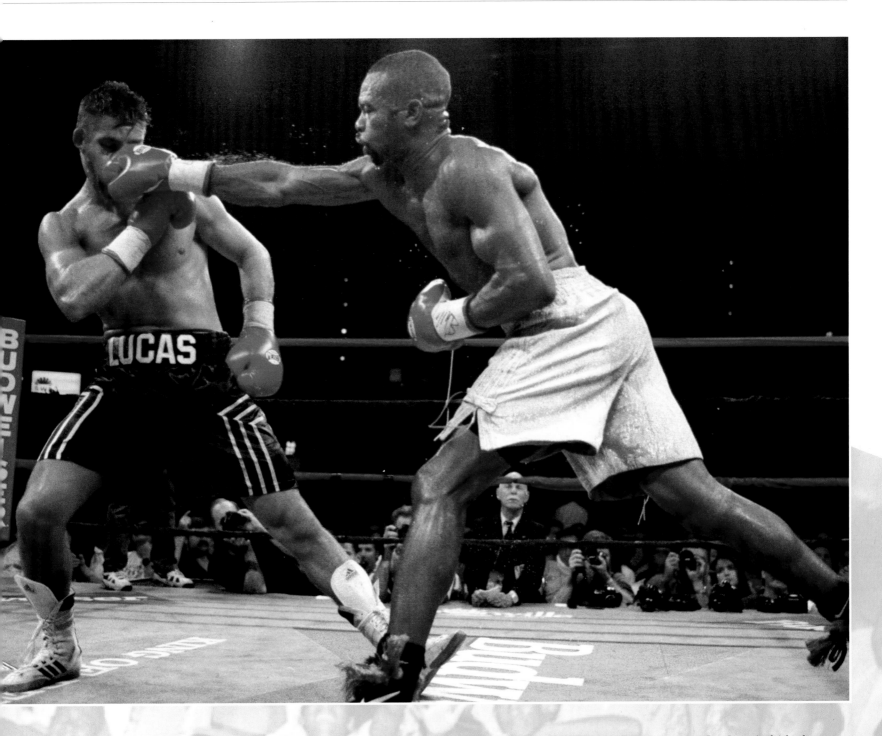

opponent. An official investigation led to the suspension of the three officials concerned – one later admitted falsifying his scorecard – and contributed to the adoption of a new scoring system at the next Olympic Games.

Despite his loss, Jones was given the Val Barker Trophy, an award bestowed upon the outstanding boxer of each Olympics. This official recognition of the flawed nature of his defeat did little to alleviate his bitterness at the result. For some time, Jones considered quitting the sport. However, he eventually began training again and in May 1989 began his professional career with a second-round stoppage victory over Ricky Randall.

Jones's main attribute as a fighter was his extraordinary speed. However, he also possessed considerable power and the early years of his career

Roy Jones (right) lands a punch to the face of Eric Lucas during a 1996 defence of his IBF super middleweight crown. Jones would defend the title one more time before moving up to light heavyweight.

JONES

The fight between Roy Jones Jr and James Toney that took place on 18 November 1994 pitted two undefeated champions against one another. A product of the famed Kronk gym in Detroit, Toney had won the IBF middleweight title in 1991 by coming from behind to beat the holder Michael Nunn. Toney had proved an active and dominant champion, beating credible challengers such as Mike McCallum and Reggie Johnson before moving up to super middleweight and beginning a second reign in the higher division. Toney was known to be a wild character out of the ring, but inside it he was a disciplined and formidable opponent.

Jones came into the fight with Toney with a perfect record of 26 wins and no defeats, but some observers still doubted whether a truly great fighter lay behind the flashy veneer. With 44 wins and two draws in 46 fights, Toney seemed to be an ideal yardstick by which to judge Jones's true worth.

Theoretically, the two fighters came into the ring evenly matched in size, with Jones just 0.45kg (1lb) heavier. However, between the weigh-in and the actual fight, Toney had put on a staggering 7.7kg (17lb) through rehydration. Normally, a weight gain of this magnitude would give the heavier fighter the advantage, but here it seemed to count against Toney as he struggled to land a punch on his quicker opponent. For round after round, Jones used his superior speed to dodge Toney's strikes while launching and landing countless punches of his own from unorthodox angles. The most memorable moments of the fight came in the third round when Jones mocked Toney by sticking out his chin, daring his opponent to hit him. When Toney mimicked him seconds later, Jones landed a perfect left hook to score a knockdown.

In the end, all three judges awarded the contest to Jones by a wide margin. Toney never fought at super middleweight again. The high and low points of a chequered career would come 11 years later, when a 106kg (233lb) incarnation of the fighter defeated John Ruiz to win the world heavyweight title, only to be stripped of his crown when a drugs test proved positive.

Roy Jones Jr delivers a left hook to the head of James Toney in November, 1994. The contest was Jones's first title fight at super middleweight.

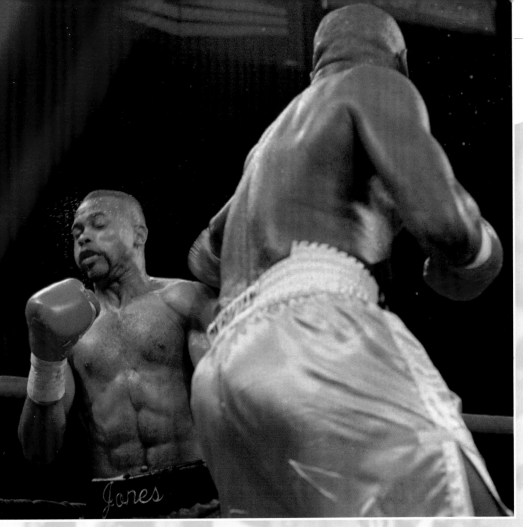

opponent with his skill in the first round before knocking him out in the second. Jones now moved up to super middleweight (76kg or 168lb) to challenge reigning champion James Toney.

After defeating Toney to claim a world title in a second weight class, Jones solidified his standing in the game with a series of easy wins. His first challenger, Antoine Byrd, was destroyed in a single round. Vinny Pazienza lasted until the sixth, but was then knocked down three times, forcing the referee to call a halt to the contest. Tony Thornton was dispatched in just three rounds, Merqui Sosa two.

Such dramatic victories would normally endear a fighter to the boxing media, but Jones's attitude to the sport riled some observers. He often expressed his boredom with boxing and threatened to quit it to pursue a career in basketball. His less than total commitment was at its most obvious in the build-up to his fight with Eric Lucas in June 1996, when he took part in a

Roy Jones (left) reacts to a punch from Mike McCallum in a contest in November, 1996. Jones beat the Jamaican veteran by decision.

Roy Jones throws a punch at Montell Griffin, despite the fact that Griffin is already on one knee. The act led to Jones being disqualified. He lost his unbeaten record in the process.

were characterized by early-round knockouts. Eventually, when champion James Toney vacated the International Boxing Federation (IBF) middleweight (73kg or 160lb) crown, Jones was given the chance to fight for the title. His opponent would be Bernard Hopkins.

Jones and Hopkins would become two of the most successful fighters of the next 10 years, but when they met in Washington DC on 22 May 1993, neither had boxed for a world title before. Their lack of big-fight experience may have led to the cautious nature of the opening rounds, when each boxer appeared to be wary of the other's ability. As the fight wore on, both became more aggressive, with Jones landing the greater number of punches. After 12 rounds the judges gave Jones a clear decision win to make him the new middleweight champion of the world.

Jones followed his victory over Hopkins with wins in three non-title fights before he defended his middleweight crown against Thomas Tate. Jones delivered an impressive performance, bewildering his

competitive basketball match on the day of his contest. Jones's exertions on behalf of the Jacksonville Barracudas seemed to have little impact on his fighting ability as he cruised to a 12-round stoppage victory.

Jones fought once more at super middleweight, before moving up to light heavyweight (79kg or 175lb), gaining the World Boxing Council (WBC) version of the title by beating Mike McCallum in November 1996. The following March, Jones defended the title against Montell Griffin. Jones's record now stood at 34 wins and no defeats, and although Griffin was also undefeated, few expected him to trouble the champion. However, for the first eight rounds the bout was evenly contested. In the ninth, Jones began to assert himself, rocking Griffin with a series of shots before knocking him down. Jones then followed up with two punches while Griffin was on his knees. The illegal move earned him a disqualification and a first defeat. A rematch with Griffin

Antonio Tarver tumbles through the ropes during the course of his second fight with Roy Jones Jr. Tarver recovered from the mishap to win a decision victory.

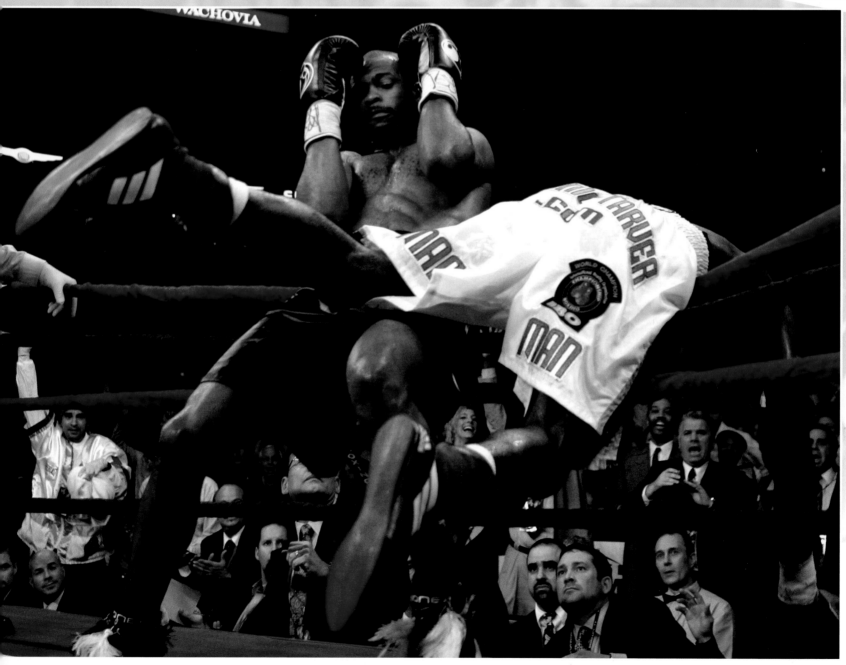

was quickly arranged for August, and Jones wasted little time in avenging his defeat, knocking his opponent out in the first round.

Between 1998 and 2002 Jones continued to defend his WBC light heavyweight crown, picking up another five different versions of the title in the process. During this period he was frequently criticized for the quality of opposition he faced and the manner in which he seemed to merely cruise to victory.

Jones clearly needed a fresh challenge and he received it in March 2003 when he moved up in weight yet again to fight John Ruiz for the World Boxing Association (WBA) heavyweight title. Victory would be truly historic: the last former middleweight to claim the heavyweight title had been Robert Fitzsimmons, who had performed the feat in 1897, only shortly after the

Roy Jones lies unconscious in the ring after being knocked out by Glen Johnson in 2004. The result was a huge shock.

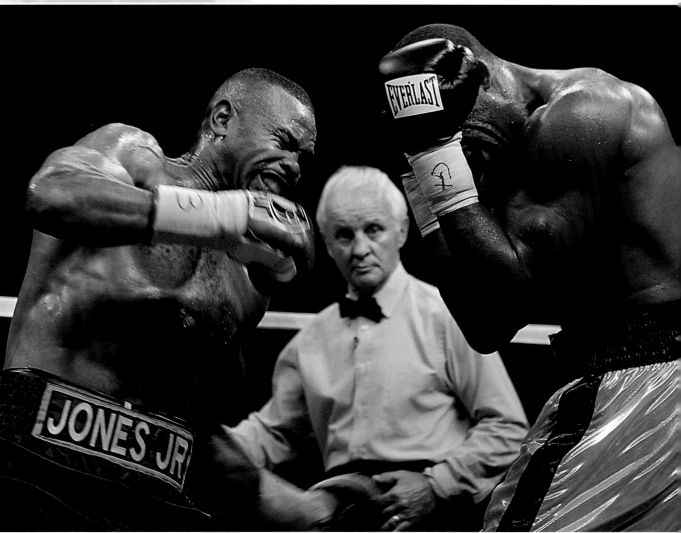

Roy Jones (left) throws a body shot at Prince Badi Ajamu during the course of his comeback win in July, 2006. Jones had lost his previous three contests.

In January 2008, a 39-year-old Roy Jones (right) took on fellow veteran Felix Trinidad in a non-title fight at Madison Square Garden, New York. Jones won a comfortable decision.

Welshman Joe Calzaghe (left) lands a right hand to the face of Roy Jones Jr in their fight in November, 2008. Calzaghe won a decision victory to preserve his unbeaten record.

end of the bare knuckle era. Jones gave up a vast amount of weight – 15kg or 33lb – but used his superior mobility to earn a clear decision victory.

The win over Ruiz, achieved at age 34, was a high point in an already great career. Jones's descent from this pinnacle was as rapid as it was unexpected. Rather than defend the heavyweight crown, he came down to light heavyweight to fight the relatively unrated Antonio Tarver in November. An unimpressive Jones escaped with a controversial majority decision win. Further ignominy came in the rematch when Jones was stopped in just two rounds. A comeback fight against Glen Johnson in September 2004 ended in a knockout defeat, while a loss against Tarver in the rubber match of their series left the formerly unbeatable Jones with a record of three losses in three matches.

Jones managed to resurrect his career in 2006, 2007 and 2008 with wins over Prince Badi Ajamu, Anthony Hanshaw and fellow veteran Felix Trinidad, but in November 2008 he came up against the unbeaten Welshman Joe Calzaghe. For once, it was Jones's turn to be bewildered by speed, and he was badly cut on the way to a lopsided decision defeat. The loss signalled that Jones's lengthy career was nearing its end, but did little to dent his reputation as one of the greatest boxers of his generation.

Roy Jones (left) absorbs further punishment from the hands of Joe Calzaghe. Jones was badly cut during the course of the fight, but survived until the final bell.

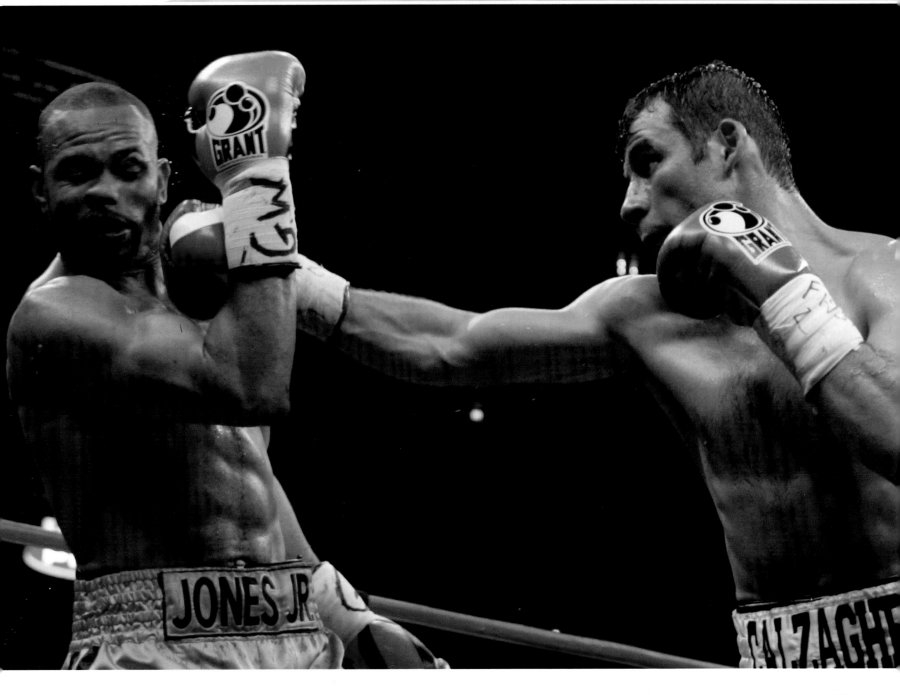

Oscar De La Hoya

A charismatic fighter whose appeal reached far beyond traditional boxing circles, Oscar De La Hoya was the sport's biggest star during the 1990s. In 2001, the establishment of Golden Boy Promotions enabled the Mexican-American to simultaneously pursue an equally successful career outside the ring. Switching constantly between the normally incompatible roles of fighter and promoter, he became one of the most influential figures in boxing.

Oscar De La Hoya was born on 4 February 1973 in southern California. Both his father and grandfather had been boxers, and with the former's backing, the young Oscar entered his first gym at age six. After more than 200 amateur contests, with all but five ending in victory, De La Hoya headed to Barcelona, where he became the only US boxer to win gold at the 1992 Olympic Games.

The backdrop to De La Hoya's Olympic success was a story that appeared to have been written by a Hollywood scriptwriter. De La Hoya had lost his mother to breast cancer in 1990, and his victory had fulfilled a promise that he had made to her while she was dying. His family history helped endear him to the American public at large. In addition, his film-star looks gained him a young female following that would not normally have been attracted to the fight game.

Considerable excitement accompanied De La Hoya's professional debut on 23 November 1992. In many ways the atmosphere echoed that which had surrounded the debut fight of another former Olympian almost 16 years earlier. Like Sugar Ray Leonard, De La Hoya was able to translate his high profile into hard currency. The young Mexican-American earned $200,000 for his defeat of Lamar Williams. The contest lasted just one minute and 42 seconds, De La Hoya winning by knockout.

The fighter now known as the "Golden Boy" was extremely active during 1993. Nine fights resulted in nine victories, eight inside the distance. All but one of

Oscar De La Hoya holds his gold medal aloft at a presentation ceremony at the 1992 Olympic Games. De La Hoya won the lightweight category.

these fights were held at lightweight (61kg or 135lb), but in March 1994 De La Hoya came down in weight to fight for the World Boxing Organization (WBO) super featherweight (59kg or 130lb) title. His opponent was the Dane Jimmy Bredahl. Although he had been a professional for less than two years, De La Hoya outclassed the champion to win by referee stoppage at the end of the 10th round.

De La Hoya's career at super featherweight lasted only a few months. He successfully defended the title once before moving up to his more natural division of lightweight to fight Jorge Paez for the vacant WBO title. It proved to be another easy night's work for De La Hoya as he won by knockout in one round and 39 seconds.

The new champion defended the title twice before the end of the year.

When De La Hoya celebrated his 22nd birthday on 4 February 1995, he did so as a two-time world champion, superficially an incredible achievement. However, both of his titles had come from the WBO, the least highly regarded of the four major governing bodies. In order to be seen as a true world champion, he would have to fight a higher class of opponent.

The first of these tougher fights would happen later that month, when De La Hoya took on the rugged Puerto Rican veteran John John Molina. Molina was knocked down in the first round, but came back strongly to turn the match into an ugly and bruising encounter. The fight

Oscar De La Hoya (right) throws a right hook at Darryl Tyson during their contest in February, 1996. It was De La Hoya's first fight at light welterweight; he won by second-round knockout.

131

was not one of De La Hoya's most spectacular displays, but by coming through to win a unanimous 12-round decision, De La Hoya proved that he was capable of carving out gutsy victories when he needed to. In May, De La Hoya added the International Boxing Federation (IBF) lightweight belt to its WBO equivalent by beating Rafael Ruelas by second-round stoppage.

De La Hoya defended his lightweight belt twice before moving up to junior welterweight (64kg or 140lb). He scored one easy victory against Darryl Tyson, before taking on one of the legends of the sport, Julio Cesar Chavez. The matchup had huge significance both in Mexico and amongst Hispanic communities in the United States. Although De La Hoya had a large Latino following, many hardcore Mexican-American fight fans were suspicious of him. With his good looks and his wholesome image, he was the antithesis of the type of fighter they traditionally took to their hearts. The fighter who most exemplified the traditional Mexican warrior was Chavez, by now a veteran of 98 fights.

The much awaited clash took place on 7 June 1996. Although the fight was held in the United States rather than Mexico, Chavez seemed to have the support of the majority of the crowd. His fans were quickly silenced,

Referee Joe Cortez calls a halt to the 1996 bout between Oscar De La Hoya and Julio Cesar Chavez (right) due to cuts. A dejected Chavez walks away.

Oscar De La Hoya (left) aims a right hand at the badly bleeding face of Julio Cesar Chavez during their first contest in 1996. The veteran Chavez was cut in the early stages of the fight.

however. Almost immediately, a jab from De La Hoya opened up a cut over Chavez's left eye. By the fourth round, the damage had worsened considerably. A doctor's inspection at the break brought the fight to a conclusion, much to the anger of Chavez, who refused to acknowledge the result as a genuine defeat.

The win over Chavez gained De La Hoya yet another belt, the World Boxing Council (WBC) title at junior welterweight. He defended the crown once before moving up in weight once more to fight Pernell Whitaker for the WBC title at welterweight (67kg or 147lb). Like Chavez, Whitaker was a genuine great, but one who was fast approaching veteran status. Nevertheless, his defensive skills were enough to frustrate De La Hoya, who emerged from the 12 rounds with a decision victory that seemed clearer to the judges than to many of the fans who watched the fight.

De La Hoya appeared to have at last found his natural weight category and remained at welterweight for the next four years. Four successful title defences followed before De La Hoya once again took on Chavez. Determined to prove a point to both his opponent and

Oscar De La Hoya (right) lands a right to the face of Pernell Whitaker during their fight in April, 1997. Despite being down in the ninth round, De La Hoya won a decision victory.

his critics, De La Hoya elected to stand and trade punches with Chavez rather than use his speed and skill to outbox him. Uncharacteristically, De La Hoya seemed intent on humiliating Chavez, and got his wish when the Mexican's corner threw in the towel at the end of the eighth round.

By the beginning of 1999, the welterweight division was dominated by four names: De La Hoya, Whitaker, Ike Quartey and Felix Trinidad. The quartet clashed over the space of eight days in February, with De La Hoya fighting the Ghanaian Quartey on the 13th and Trinidad taking on Whitaker exactly one week later. Both matches pitted veterans against fighters in their prime, and in both instances youth prevailed, though in De La Hoya's case it was a close run thing. Quartey dominated the early stages of the fight, and a spirited comeback by the Golden Boy only convinced two of the three judges that he had won the fight.

The two victories set up a showdown between Trinidad and De La Hoya, two undefeated champions of almost the same age. De La Hoya started the fight impressively and by the end of the ninth round

Oscar De La Hoya (left) goes on the attack against Germany's Felix Sturm in their 2004 middleweight bout. De La Hoya won a close and controversial decision.

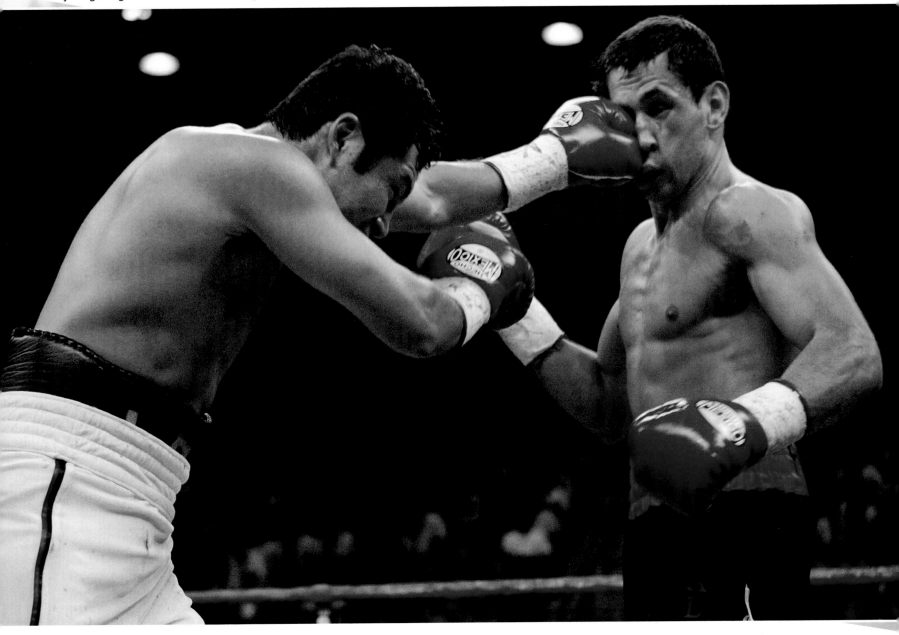

135

DE LA HOYA

VARGAS

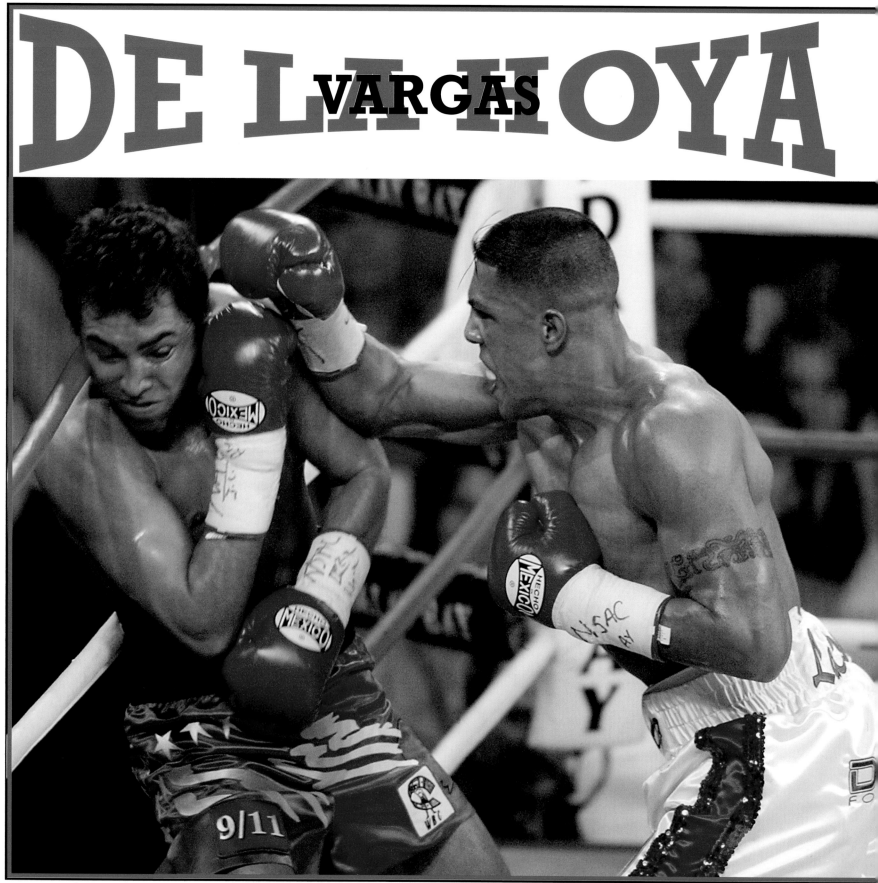

While boxers often exaggerate ill feeling towards their opponents as part of a calculated attempt to increase ticket sales, occasionally a fight occurs where the participants do genuinely hate one another. That was certainly the case when Oscar De La Hoya took on Fernando Vargas in Las Vegas on 14 September 2002. Like De La Hoya, Vargas was a Mexican-American who hailed from southern California. He had been attempting to lure De La Hoya into the ring for several years, mainly by hurling insults at him, questioning his courage, manhood and whether he was truly worthy to represent the Mexican people in the ring. Bizarrely, the animosity seemed to trace back to an earlier incident at a training camp, when De La Hoya laughed when Vargas fell over in the snow while jogging. Whatever the origins of the feud, it was real enough by the time of the fight, with Vargas publicly stating that he would rather die in the ring than lose to his detested opponent.

Many question marks surrounded De La Hoya as he entered the contest. He had not stepped into the ring for almost 15 months and now faced potential distractions in his new role as promoter. Two of his previous five contests had ended in defeat and he had only fought at junior middleweight (70kg or 154lb) once before. Initially, it seemed as if the latter problem might prove to be his biggest worry. The physically stronger Vargas bulldozed him into the ropes in the first round in an attempt to turn the fight into a close-quarter war, but De La Hoya responded well, using his experience to ensure that the contest took place in the centre of the ring, where his greater speed and boxing ability would tell.

By the middle of the 10th round, De La Hoya seemed to have a narrow lead, and the matter was settled almost beyond doubt when a short left hook caught Vargas just before the bell. He had still not recovered fully by the beginning of the 11th, and another left hook knocked him to the canvas. The younger man bravely got back to his feet, but the fight was stopped seconds later.

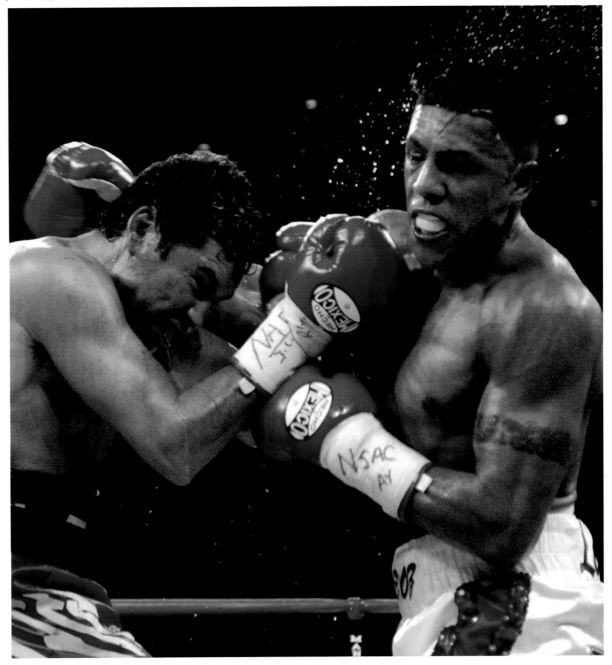

Fernando Vargas (right) traps Oscar De La Hoya against the ropes during the course of their 2002 grudge match. As well as personal pride, the world light middleweight title was also at stake.

Sweat flies off the head of Fernando Vargas (right) after a punch from Oscar De La Hoya. De La Hoya eventually won their fight in the 11th round.

appeared to have built up a convincing lead. His dominance was so great that his corner advised him to take no risks in the final three rounds. It proved to be a fatal mistake. De La Hoya spent nine minutes dancing out of range, allowing the Puerto Rican to steal the rounds and claim a controversial majority decision victory.

De La Hoya came back from the loss to Trinidad with a seventh-round victory over Derrell Coley, but then ran into trouble again when he fought Shane Mosley, a former world champion at lightweight with an unbeaten record stretching back seven years. For once, De La Hoya found himself to be the slower fighter and Mosley's dominance of the second half of the fight earned him a split-decision victory.

In 2001 De La Hoya scored wins over Arturo Gatti and Javier Castillejo, but the year was more significant for developments outside the ring. De La Hoya founded Golden Boy Promotions, a company that aimed to give boxers a greater control of their careers and tap into

One of the toughest fights of Oscar De La Hoya's career came in 2004, when he took on long-standing middleweight champion Bernard Hopkins. The naturally bigger and stronger Hopkins stopped De La Hoya in the ninth round.

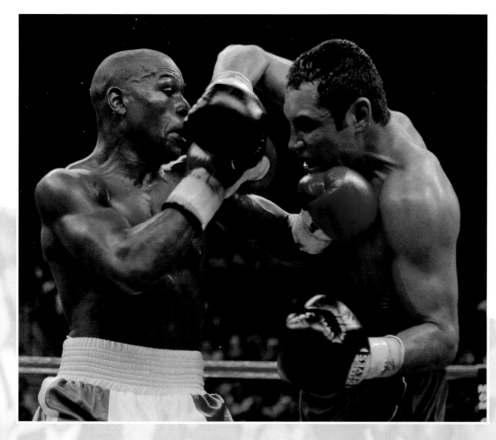

on the line – and set up a money-spinning encounter with long-term champion Bernard Hopkins later that year. Hopkins, however, proved to be too strong, stopping De La Hoya in the ninth round, the first non-decision defeat of the Mexican-American's career.

After the loss to Hopkins, De La Hoya took more than 18 months off, coming back to beat Ricardo Mayorga, another boxer who turned his contest with De La Hoya into a grudge match by showering him with abuse. Then, following a year's lay-off, De La Hoya came up against the man who was now widely regarded as the best pound-for-pound fighter in the sport: Floyd Mayweather Jr. The younger and quicker Mayweather won by split decision.

Although it counted as a loss on his resumé, De La Hoya's match with Mayweather proved that he could still compete at the very highest level. His next superfight, however, had the opposite effect. His December 2008 showdown with Manny Pacquiao ended in humiliating fashion when De La Hoya quit on his stool after the end of the eighth round. However, in one way, De La Hoya ended up profiting even from this defeat. Pacquiao was now an even greater superstar and Golden Boy Promotions would be overseeing his next fight.

Floyd Mayweather (left) and Oscar De La Hoya trade punches in the 10th round of their clash in May, 2007. The contest was close; Mayweather won on a split decision.

Many media pundits thought that Manny Pacquiao (right) would be too small to trouble Oscar De La Hoya, but the Filipino dominated their 2008 fight. De La Hoya quit after the eighth round.

the lucrative and growing Hispanic market. Initially a straightforward boxing promotions firm, Golden Boy quickly grew and diversified, investing in real estate and publishing.

In the years after the formation of Golden Boy, De La Hoya's ring appearances became more infrequent. Fights were always high profile, but led to almost as many losses as wins. De La Hoya's dual career began well with a win over hated rival Fernando Vargas in 2002, but the following year, he lost a closely contested rematch to Shane Mosley.

De La Hoya reacted to the disappointment by moving up to middleweight (73kg or 160lb), snatching a decision from the German Felix Sturm in June 2004. The victory was highly controversial, but it achieved its intended dual purpose. It gained De La Hoya a world title in a sixth weight class – Sturm's WBO belt had been

Manny Pacquiao

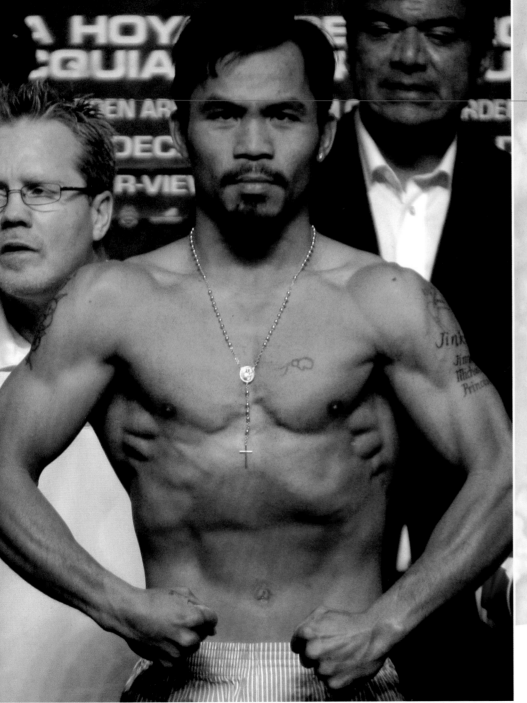

South-east Asia has a long tradition of supplying great champions to boxing's lighter weight categories. The most famous of these fighters include Khaosai Galaxy, the "Thai Tyson" who dominated the super flyweight division in the late 1980s, and the great Filipino super featherweight Gabriel "Flash" Elorde. The first Asian boxer to truly become a worldwide superstar, however, was Elorde's compatriot, Manny Pacquiao.

The idea that boxing provides a road out of poverty may be one of the great clichés of sport, but an examination of the lives of many great champions shows that it is one rooted in truth. The story of Manny Pacquiao exemplifies this more than most. He was born on 17 December 1978 in Bukidnon in the Philippines, and brought up by his single mother. The family's poverty meant that Pacquiao was denied an education, and instead spent his early childhood working to support his family. During this time he developed a love of boxing, asking Dizon Cordero, the father and trainer of a local fighter, to teach him the sport. Cordero took him in and guided him in his early amateur career.

Pacquiao's financial situation meant that he needed to fight for money as soon as possible. At age 14 he left for Manila where he found work in a factory, scraping the rust off lumps of recycled metal while searching for a gym that was prepared to take him in. His talent was soon spotted and on 22 January 1995 he fought his first professional contest, a four-round bout against Edmund Enting Ignacio. Pacquiao was effectively still a boy – he had celebrated his 16th birthday one month beforehand – but managed to outpoint his older opponent.

It did not take long for Pacquiao to gain public recognition. After two more wins he made his televized debut in July 1995, appearing on *Blow by Blow*, a Philippine boxing show. Pacquiao won by technical

Manny Pacquiao shows off his physique at the weigh-in for his 2008 fight with Oscar De La Hoya. The contest was Pacquiao's first at welterweight.

knockout in the second round. He quickly became a popular fighter, the combination of his boyish looks and aggressive style endearing him to fans. In Pacquiao's 12th contest, this lack of emphasis on defence cost him dearly when he was knocked out by Rustico Torrecampo. However, the defeat proved to be a temporary lapse.

Pacquiao's first shot at a title came in June 1997 when he took on the Thai Chokchai Chockvivat for the Oriental Pacific Boxing Federation (OPBF) flyweight (51kg or 112lb) crown. Pacquiao won with a fifth-round knockout. In his first defence of the title he took even less time to dispatch another Thai, Panomdej Ohyuthanakorn, winning in just one minute and 38 seconds of the first round. These victories set Pacquiao up for a chance to secure a world title.

Pacquiao's opponent would be yet another Thai, Chatchai Sasakul. Chatchai would pose a far greater challenge than his two countrymen. The technically superior boxer, the Thai dominated the first six rounds. In the seventh, however, a straight left from Pacquiao altered the course of the contest. Pacquiao upped his aggression and knocked his opponent unconscious in the eighth to claim his first world title.

Pacquiao's first reign as world champion was short. He failed to make weight for his second title defence, against Medgoen Singsurat in September 1999, and then lost the match by way of a third-round knockout. He promptly moved up to junior featherweight (or super bantamweight: 55kg or 122lb) and won his next six contests. In June 2001 he was rewarded with a fight against Lehlohonolo Ledwaba for the International Boxing Federation (IBF) title at his new weight. Aside from its title status, the fight was also important because it gave Pacquiao the opportunity to fight in the United States for the first time. The Filipino boxer seized the opportunity to increase his profile and marketability by winning by a sixth-round technical knockout.

From this point onward, Pacquiao would increasingly fight on the other side of the Pacific from his homeland. The move had no adverse affect on his status as a national hero. His already considerable popularity

Manny Pacquiao (right) is pictured with Lehlohonolo Ledwaba of South Africa after their clash in Las Vegas in June, 2001. Pacquiao's victory won him the IBF super bantamweight title. It also introduced his explosive style to US audiences.

Mexico's Juan Manuel Marquez (right) goes on the offensive against Manny Pacquiao in the pair's first encounter in May, 2004. Marquez was knocked down three times in the first round, but came back to claim a draw.

increased to astronomical levels. City streets would be deserted on the nights of his fights, while victories were marked by lavish civic celebrations, as politicians fought amongst themselves to be associated with him.

To the boxing public outside the Philippines, Pacquiao's reputation was cemented by a series of fights against a trio of truly great Mexican boxers: Marco Antonio Barrera, Erik Morales and Juan Manuel Marquez. Pacquiao defended his super bantamweight title four times before stepping up to featherweight (57kg or 126lb) to fight Barrera in a non-title contest in November 2003. Barrera went into the bout as favourite, mainly on account of his greater experience of fighting at the higher weight limit. The pre-fight wisdom appeared to be correct when Pacquiao went down in the first round, but he recovered to inflict a knockdown of

A bloodied Manny Pacquiao (left) crashes a left hand into the face of Erik Morales in March, 2005. Pacquiao lost the fight, but would gain his revenge the following year.

his own in the third. For the remainder of the fight Pacquiao swarmed over Barrera, inflicting considerable damage. The end came in the 11th when the Mexican's trainer stepped into the ring to force the referee to stop the fight.

Pacquiao's performance against Barrera earned him a title fight against Juan Manuel Marquez. The first three minutes of the contest suggested that it would be an easy night's work for the Filipino: Marquez went down three times before the end of the first round. However, the champion rallied and managed to win enough rounds over the course of the remainder of the bout to secure a draw.

After the disappointment of the Marquez fight, Pacquiao headed back to the Philippines, where he defeated Narongrit Pirang. Returning to the United States, Pacquiao then embarked on a trio of fights with Erik Morales. The first, held in Las Vegas on 19 March

Manny Pacquiao (right) slips a right hand through the defences of Hector Velazquez in 2005. Velazquez was just one of a succession of Mexicans beaten by Pacquiao around this time.

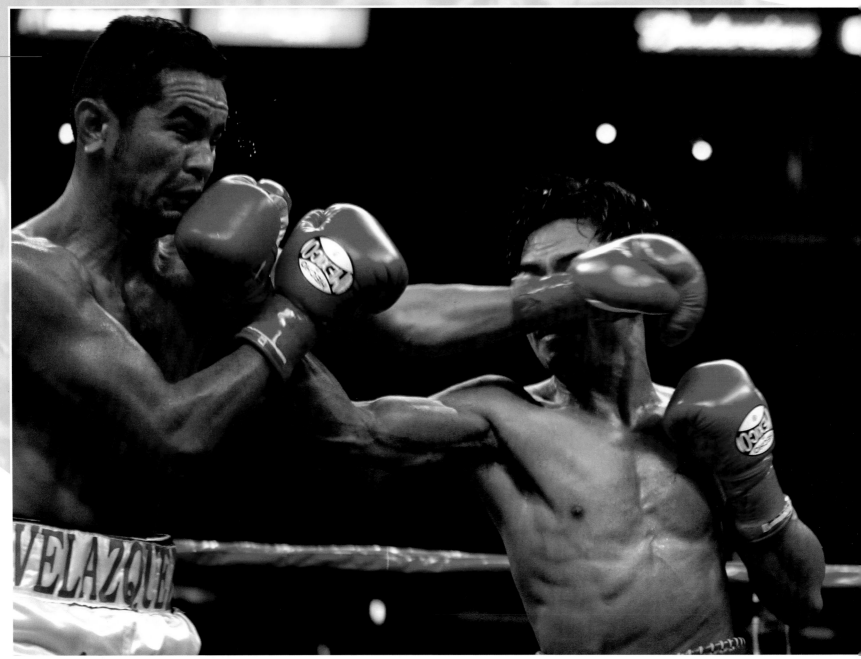

2005, resulted in a close decision victory for the Mexican. Morales controlled most of the contest, but the most memorable aspect of the fight was an epic final round in which a bloodied Pacquiao, behind on points, chased the knockout that would save the match.

In January 2006, after defeating another Mexican, Hector Velazquez, Pacquiao confronted Morales for the second time. Morales began strongly, but Pacquiao took over in the middle rounds and began to inflict considerable punishment. In the 10th Morales was first knocked down and then stopped, the first time that he had suffered this fate in his career. Any doubts as to who was the superior fighter were extinguished in November when Pacquiao won the rubber match of the series with a third-round knockout.

The following year Pacquiao beat Jorge Solis and handed a second defeat to Marco Antonio Barrera. But while 2007 was successful, it was in 2008 that Pacquiao truly established himself as an all-time great. The year saw him win three fights in three different weight classes, gaining two world titles in the process. The first contest was a rematch with Marquez. The fight mirrored the first encounter in that the Mexican came back strongly from an early setback, in this case a third-round knockdown. This time, however, two of the three judges gave Pacquiao the victory. Many boxing journalists did not agree with the decision, but it was enough to win Pacquiao the WBC super featherweight (59kg or 130lb) title.

In June 2008, Pacquiao took on David Diaz for the same organization's lightweight (61kg or 135lb) crown. The Filipino was utterly dominant, cutting his opponent badly before knocking him out in the ninth. He then moved up in weight yet again to fight the ageing superstar Oscar De La Hoya. Pacquiao's win in December 2008, cemented his position as the best pound-for-pound fighter in the world. He consolidated this status in May 2009 with an equally emphatic victory over the British fighter Ricky Hatton. Like De La Hoya, Hatton had spent most of his career fighting at a higher weight than the Filipino. However, Pacquiao completely dominated their brief contest, finishing it inside of two rounds with an exquisite left hook, a punch that provided a perfect example of his by now unrivalled blend of technique and power.

Manny Pacquiao (left) trades punches with Jorge Solis in their 2007 world title fight. Pacquiao knocked Solis out in the eighth round.

PACQUIAO

DE LA HOYA

By the middle of 2008 Manny Pacquiao was undoubtedly the hottest fighter in the sport. For the previous two years boxing writers had debated whether he or Floyd Mayweather Jr deserved to be seen as the world's best pound-for-pounder. The retirement of Mayweather in the same month that Pacquiao claimed the lightweight title from David Diaz settled the argument. Pacquiao was not only good, he was popular as well. The United States public had taken the fighter they knew as the "Pac-Man" to their hearts. The second Marquez fight earned 400,000 pay-per-view buys, an astonishing amount for a fighter from one of the lighter weight categories.

One of the few boxers who could rival Pacquiao's popularity was Oscar De La Hoya. Although he had lost three of his previous six contests, the multiple world champion was still a huge draw. Talk of a fight between Pacquiao and De La Hoya had begun as early as March, but had been dismissed as a joke by many boxing journalists. After all, Pacquiao had begun his career as a 48kg (106lb) mini-flyweight, while De La Hoya had fought as high as

Manny Pacquiao (right) prepares to throw a punch at a defensive Oscar De La Hoya in 2008. Pacquiao's upset win consolidated his superstar status.

Manny Pacquiao celebrates his win over Oscar De La Hoya in their welterweight clash in December 2008. In the background a member of Pacquiao's entourage holds the WBC lightweight belt that he had won earlier in the year.

middleweight (73kg or 160lb). However, as the months drew on, fewer and fewer people seemed willing to condemn the match as a freak show. Some pundits even suggested that Pacquiao might have a chance of winning.

Almost no one, however, predicted the utter demolition that occurred in the MGM Grand Arena, Las Vegas, on 6 December 2008. Fighting for the first time at welterweight (67kg or 147lb), Pacquiao proved not only the quicker fighter, as had been expected, but the more powerful too. For eight rounds he hit De La Hoya almost at will, building up an insurmountable lead on the judges' scorecards. The display was enough to force De La Hoya's corner to throw in the towel. At the beginning of the ninth, the outclassed Mexican-American got up from his stool and walked over to congratulate his opponent. The gesture seemed to signal the end of De La Hoya's career as a serious force in world boxing, and a passing of his mantle to the biggest attraction in the sport.

David Diaz shows the effects of his mauling at the hands of Manny Pacquiao. Diaz was cut in the early stages of their 2008 fight and finally stopped in the ninth round.

Boxing in the 21st Century

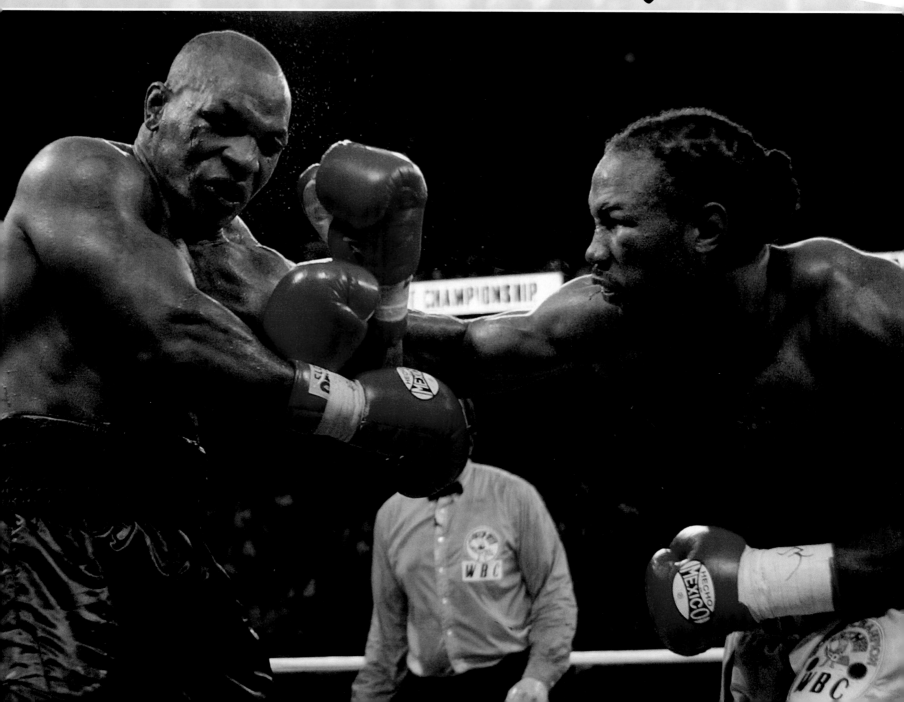

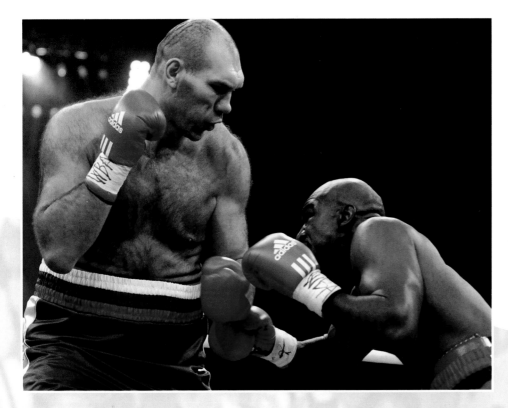

Boxing entered the twenty-first century at something of a crossroads. It faced numerous problems, prompting a succession of media commentators to predict its decline. However, despite its difficulties, the sport continued to produce a host of charismatic fighters and dramatic contests.

The main problem facing boxing at the beginning of this century was the confusing number of organizations that claimed to run the sport. The issue was not a new one. Ever since 1963, the World Boxing Association (WBA) and World Boxing Council (WBC) had named their own champions. However, the arrival of the International Boxing Federation (IBF) in 1983 and World Boxing Organization (WBO) in 1988 further muddied the waters. At least a dozen other similarly titled bodies arrived over the course of the next two decades. The situation left casual fans of the sport unsure who the real champions actually were. It also resulted in secondary negative effects. Political issues often prevented top fighters from competing against one another, and the lack of clear title bouts caused mainstream media coverage to decline.

The giant Nikolay Valuev (left) was the most recognizable of the new breed of Eastern European fighters who dominated the heavyweight scene in the early twenty-first century. Here he towers over Evander Holyfield in their WBA title fight in 2008.

Lennox Lewis (right) delivers a punch to the side of Mike Tyson's head during the course of their fight in 2002. Lewis's win confirmed his position as the top heavyweight in the world.

Wladimir Klitschko (left) throws a left jab at Sultan Ibragimov in a 2008 fight between the WBO and IBF heavyweight champions. Klitschko won the contest to unite the two titles.

The problem of multiple champions hurt the heavyweight division more than most. For large parts of the twentieth century, it had been ruled by a single fighter who was instantly recognizable throughout the world. Dempsey, Louis, Marciano, Ali and Tyson were larger-than-life figures who were familiar even to members of the public who had no real interest in the fight game. Towards the end of the 1990s, one fighter did seem to be establishing the kind of dominance that these figures had enjoyed in their prime. The British/Canadian Lennox Lewis had won the WBC crown in 1993, but had only gained widespread recognition as the best fighter in the division six years later after his victory over Evander Holyfield. His status was solidified by an emphatic win over Mike Tyson in 2002.

However, he defended his title only once, and his retirement in February 2004 left the heavyweight scene hugely fragmented.

In the early years of this century, a succession of men laid claim to the title of world heavyweight champion. They included a number of fighters from Eastern Europe: Oleg Maskaev, Ruslan Chagaev, Serguei Lyahkhovich, Sultan Ibragimov and Nikolay Valuev among them. Other heavyweight champions included John Ruiz, Chris Byrd, Corrie Sanders and Shannon Briggs. For one reason or another, none of these men truly established himself as the best heavyweight fighter in the world, although one did make history. At 2.13m (7ft) and 149kg (328lb), Valuev was both the tallest and the heaviest fighter ever to claim a world title.

Samuel Peter (left) winces in pain as a shot from Vitali Klitschko lands on his jaw. Klitschko beat Peter in October, 2008 to join his brother Wladimir as a world heavyweight champion.

Bernard Hopkins (left) takes evasive action as Welshman Joe Calzaghe goes on the attack in their bout in April, 2008. Calzaghe would retire undefeated 10 months later.

Bernard Hopkins (right) would bounce back from his loss to Joe Calzaghe to defeat Kelly Pavlik six months later. The veteran Hopkins completely outclassed his younger opponent.

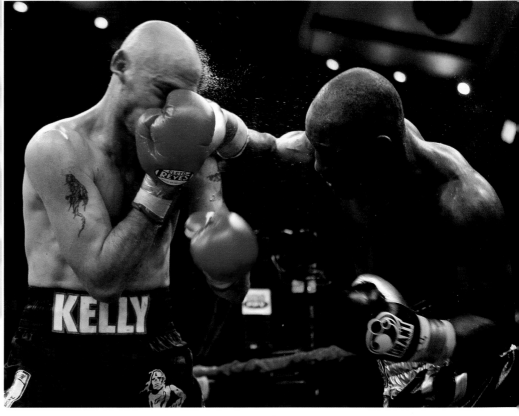

At the beginning of 2008 it looked unlikely that the heavyweight division would be dominated by one man in the immediate future. By the end of the year, however, it was at least controlled by one family. Between 2000 and 2003 Wladimir Klitschko had enjoyed a two-and-a half-year reign as the WBO champion. His career had been derailed by two stoppage losses, but he returned to form in 2006, winning the IBF title by beating Chris Byrd. In February 2008 he reclaimed the WBO title with a win over Sultan Ibragimov.

During this period, Wladimir had been helped by his elder brother Vitali, who had himself enjoyed two stints as a world title holder. Persistent knee injuries had eventually forced him to retire, but in October 2008 he returned to the ring after a lay-off of nearly four years. A generous WBC allowed him to compete for a world title in his first fight back and he repaid their faith in him by completely outclassing a sluggish Samuel Peter. Two months later Wladimir looked equally composed in beating Hasim Rahman. The twin victories left three of the four major world titles in the hands of the Klitschko family.

The rise of the Klitschkos was emblematic of another trend that was transforming boxing. During the first 100

years of boxing's history, most of the sport's most celebrated fighters had hailed from the United States. This situation began to change in the early twenty-first century. By the end of 2008, a relatively small percentage of the boxers listed in *The Ring* magazine's ranking lists hailed from the US. In particular, European fighters, often derided in US boxing circles, accounted for a large number of fighters in the higher weight classes.

Low attendances for some high-profile fights in the US have been offered by some journalists as evidence for the death of boxing. However, the sport has been flourishing elsewhere. On 3 November 2007 more than 50,000 fans gathered in Cardiff's Millennium Stadium to watch a Welshman fight a Dane. The Welshman was Joe Calzaghe, one of the sport's longest serving champions. He had begun his reign as the WBO super middleweight

(76kg or 168lb) champion in October 1997, with a win over Chris Eubank. Some 10 years later he remained unbeaten. Calzaghe's Danish opponent was Mikkel Kessler, the WBA and WBC champion at the same weight. The fight provided further evidence of Calzaghe's boxing ability as he used his greater speed and skill to win a comfortable decision.

The win over Kessler was Calzaghe's 21st and final defence of his WBO title. Then in 2008 he moved up to light heavyweight (79kg or 175lb) to fight two veteran Americans, Bernard Hopkins and Roy Jones Jr. Both contests resulted in wins for the Welshman. The victory over Hopkins was a scrappy affair that was loudly contested by the loser. Calzaghe looked far better against Jones, winning almost every round and badly cutting the man who had once been the best pound-for-pound fighter in the world. The two wins helped to

Caught by a punch from Floyd Mayweather Jr (left), Britain's Ricky Hatton falls to the canvas. The pair fought in December, 2007 when Mayweather was generally regarded as the best pound-for-pound fighter in the world.

cement Calzaghe's reputation, leaving him with a perfect record of 46 victories and no losses, but also left some boxing fans frustrated that the contests had not happened years earlier when the fighters were closer to their peaks.

The defeat against Calzaghe was a rare lapse from Hopkins, who had been one of the most dominant middleweight champions of all time. The man who later revelled in the nickname the "Executioner" had begun boxing while in prison and did not have his first professional fight until the age of 23. Making up for lost time, he won the IBF world middleweight title in 1995 and held it until 2005, by which time he was 40 years old. The run of 20 straight title defences included wins over superstars Oscar De La Hoya and Felix Trinidad.

Hopkins's loss of his title at such an advanced age might have been expected to end his career. However, he showed surprising resilience, beating Antonio Tarver and Ronald "Winky" Wright before running into Calzaghe. A second contest in 2008 was widely predicted to be one step too far for the veteran. It pitched him against boxing's new golden boy, the undefeated middleweight champion Kelly Pavlik. However, Hopkins was not daunted by either the reputation of his opponent or the 17-year age gap between them. The older man drew on all of his experience to completely dominate the contest.

Pavlik's fight with Hopkins had been a non-title affair at light heavyweight, so Pavlik went into 2009 with his status as a world title holder intact. He was in possession

Antonio Margarito (right) follows up his knockdown of Miguel Cotto with a right hook. Margarito's win in the pair's 2008 welterweight title fight seemed to mark him out as a future star. However, he lost the crown to Shane Mosley the following year.

of the WBC and WBO belts. The other two major versions of the title resided in Germany. The WBA title was held by Felix Sturm, while the IBF crown was in the hands of the unbeaten Arthur Abraham, a Berlin-based Armenian who had built up a reputation in his adopted homeland for his entertainingly aggressive style.

In the early years of the twenty-first century a number of men had vied for the unofficial title of best pound-for-pound boxer in the world. They included Roy Jones Jr, Bernard Hopkins and Sugar Shane Mosley. By 2006, however, the choice was between two men, both from boxing's lighter weight divisions. The first was the tough and charismatic Filipino Manny Pacquiao. The other was Floyd Mayweather Jr.

Like Pacquiao, Mayweather was a multiple world champion. Beginning his career as a 59kg (130lb) super featherweight, he methodically worked his way through the weight divisions, eventually winning titles in five different categories. Although he was one of the most skilful boxers of his generation, Mayweather became equally well known for his chaotic family life, particularly his volatile relationship with his father and sometime trainer, Floyd Sr. The younger Floyd eventually fired his father and replaced him with his uncle, prompting a bitter and complex feud that kept the family firmly in the media spotlight.

Mayweather Jr's most productive year, financially at least, was 2007, when he scored a narrow win over

Sugar Shane Mosley (right) connects with a hard right hand in his January 2009 fight against Antonio Margarito. Mosley came into the fight as a heavy underdog, but pulled off a surprise stoppage victory.

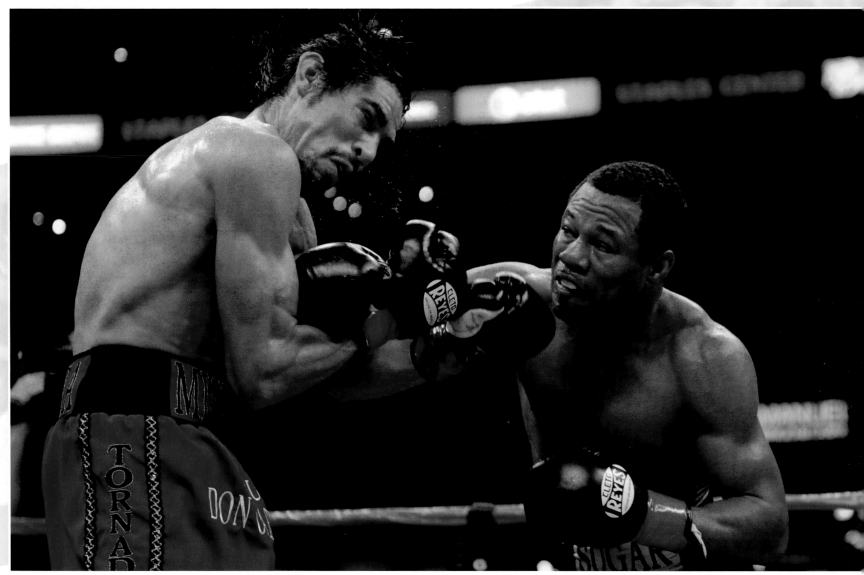

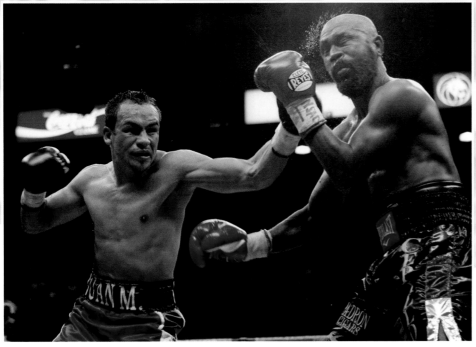

Juan Manuel Marquez throws a left hook to the jaw of Joel Casamayor en route to his 11th-round victory in September, 2008. Marquez was just one of a number of Mexican fighters to flourish in the early twenty-first century.

Puerto Rican Ivan Calderon (right) takes a punch from Hugo Cazares of Mexico in their 2007 battle for the world junior flyweight title. Calderon won the contest, and also proved victorious in the rematch.

De La Hoya at junior middleweight (70kg or 154lb), before coming down to welterweight (67kg or 147lb) to fight the unbeaten Ricky Hatton, an Englishman famous for the ferocity of his body punches. Hatton's boisterous travelling supporters made the December 2007 clash a memorable one, but Mayweather's greater class told in the end.

Mayweather quit the game, temporarily at least, the following year, but his retirement did not leave the welterweight division bereft of talent. The weight class boasted a number of excellent fighters, including Antonio Margarito, Miguel Cotto, Shane Mosley, Paul Williams and the up-and-coming Andre Berto.

The Mexican Margarito and the Puerto Rican Cotto fought an epic battle in the summer of 2008. Margarito won the contest with an 11th-round knockout to claim the WBA's divisional belt. Surprisingly, Margarito lost the title in his first defence. His conqueror was the 37-year-old Mosley, who put in the kind of performance that had propelled him to the top of the pound-for-pound ratings at the turn of the century.

The success of Cotto and Margarito signalled the continuation of one great twentieth-century boxing tradition. The lighter weight categories still featured a number of talented Hispanic fighters following in the footsteps of greats such as Alexis Arguello, Roberto Duran and Julio Cesar Chavez. Among the most notable were the Mexicans Marco Antonio Barrera, Erik Morales, Juan Manuel Marquez and Israel Vazquez, the Cuban Joel Casamayor and the Puerto Rican Ivan Calderon.

Barrera and Morales enjoyed a rivalry as great as almost any in the sport. Its ingredients included two fighters of contrasting backgrounds, a huge degree of

The rivalry between Marco Antonio Barrera and Erik Morales was one of the greatest in boxing history. Here, Morales (right) lands a punch to the face of Barrera during the course of their third contest.

personal animosity, and more than one disputed decision. The two fighters clashed three times over the course of four and a half years. Their first fight, which took place in February 2000, was conducted at a brutally frenetic pace. In a thrilling climax, Barrera knocked Morales down in the final round but, to the shock of many watching, still found himself on the wrong end of a split decision. Ironically, many thought that Morales did win the 2002 rematch, but this time the fight was awarded to Barrera.

The two controversial decisions added to the bad blood between the two men, which was rooted in class and regional differences: Barrera was the son of prosperous parents from Mexico City, while Morales has been born in poverty in the border town of Tijuana. The inevitable rubber match took place in Las Vegas on 27 November 2004. After a bad beating by Manny Pacquiao, Barrera went into the contest as the underdog.

However, opting for a strategy of all-out attack, he dominated the first half of the fight and went on to win a majority decision.

For veteran observers, the Barrera–Morales trilogy evoked memories of some of the great rivalries in boxing history: Sugar Ray Robinson's six brutal contests against Jake LaMotta, the epic Ali–Frazier series that climaxed with the "Thrilla in Manila", and Sugar Ray Leonard's legendary confrontations with Roberto Duran. Putting both their reputations and their physical health on the line, Barrera and Morales fought with phenomenal levels of heart and skill, and the back story to their rivalry merely increased the drama. Their contests personified the elemental appeal of boxing, an appeal that has seduced fans for more than 100 years. Whatever the problems facing the sport, a new generation of fighters will surely continue this grand tradition.

American champion Adrien Broner – also known as 'The Problem' – enjoying his victory over Gavin Rees from Newport, Wales, during their WBC lightweight title bout in Atlantic City, February 2013.

Index

M

N

O

P

Q

R

S

T

V

W

Acknowledgements

The publisher would like to thank the following
for their kind help and contribution:

Getty Images, UK
US Library of Congress, Washington DC, USA
Topfoto Images, UK
AP Images, USA
PA Photos, UK